INDIVIDUALIZING INSTRUCTION
FOR THE
EDUCATIONALLY HANDICAPPED

ABOUT THE AUTHOR

Jack Campbell is the *Class of 1964 Professor* in the Education Department at Mount Saint Mary's College in Emmitsburg, MD. During the Spring semester of 1995, he was visiting professor at St. Andrew's College in Scotland where he lectured, mentored, and conducted research. During the 17 years prior to 1995, he served as Provost and Vice President at Mount Saint Mary's College. From 1971 to 1978, he was a professor in the special education program at the University of Nevada.

He has published articles in such journals as *Education, Journal of Research in Education, Planning for Higher Education, Educational Record, Mental Retardation, Education and Training of the Mentally Retarded, and the Journal for Special Educators of the Mentally Retarded.*

He teaches undergraduate and graduate courses at Mount Saint Mary's in the areas of special education and educational psychology.

He earned his M.Ed. in Special Education from the University of Delaware and his Ed.D. in Special Education from The Pennsylvania State University.

INDIVIDUALIZING INSTRUCTION FOR THE EDUCATIONALLY HANDICAPPED

Teaching Strategies in Remedial and Special Education

By

JACK CAMPBELL, ED.D.

Mount Saint Mary's College
Emmitsburg, Maryland

CHARLES C THOMAS • PUBLISHER, LTD.
Springfield • Illinois • U.S.A.

Published and Distributed Throughout the World by

CHARLES C THOMAS • PUBLISHER, LTD.
2600 South First Street
Springfield, Illinois 62794-9265

© *1998 by* CHARLES C THOMAS • PUBLISHER, LTD.
ISBN 0-398-06892-5 (paper)
ISBN 0-398-06901-8 (cloth)

Library of Congress Catalog Card Number: 98-27042

With THOMAS BOOKS *careful attention is given to all details of manufacturing and design. It is the Publisher's desire to present books that are satisfactory as to their physical qualities and artistic possibilities and appropriate for their particular use.* THOMAS BOOKS *will be true to those laws of quality that assure a good name and good will.*

Printed in the United States of America
CR-R-3

Library of Congress Cataloging in Publication Data

Campbell, Jack, Ed. D.
    Individualizing instruction for the educationally handicapped :
teaching strategies in remedial and special education / by Jack
Campbell.
        p.   cm.
    Includes bibliographical references and index.
    ISBN 0-398-06892-5 (pbk.) ISBN 0-398-06901-8 (cloth)
    1. Remedial teaching. 2. Special education. 3. Handicapped
children--Education. 4. Individualized instruction. I. Title.
LB1029.R4C35   1998
371.9'043--dc21   98-27042
                                                                        CIP

This book is dedicated to David L. Campbell, teacher,
who spent a career teaching educationally handicapped children,
while I devoted a career to talking and writing about it.

and

To Robert M. Smith, mentor and friend,
who helped me develop what I needed to be able to talk and write about it.

PREFACE

At some point in a career a teacher will encounter a child who does not do well in school. The reasons for that child's lack of success can be as varied as the number of children in a class. Not only do these students not do well in school, they typically do not like school very much.

The unfortunate reality is that knowing what label has been attached to a child is not particularly helpful to the teacher. There is nothing about the term mentally retarded, learning disabled, or behavior disordered that provides the teacher with any information about how to teach the child. In fact, most children who are on the milder end of the continuum of mental retardation, learning disabilities, and behavior disorders have more in common with each other than they do with others who share the same label. It may well be better to simply consider these children to be educationally handicapped because their problems, most typically, only manifest themselves in school.

Many of these children qualify for special education and most often are integrated into the regular classroom for a significant portion of the school day. When they are not in the regular classroom, they are being provided special education in a resource room or some other pull-out program. In addition to these special education students, the term educationally handicapped may well include that multitude of children who are just on the cusp. There are many children who do not qualify for special education but whose academic performance is consistently below the average of the group on a host of school-related variables.

The reasons for educationally handicapped children's underachievement and discomfort in the school setting are legion. Most importantly, the reasons are different for virtually each and every educationally handicapped child. Said another way, educationally handicapped children are a very heterogeneous population, and as such, require individualized educational programs if they are to catch up academically and begin enjoying the school experience.

In order to be successful at individualizing instruction, it is incumbent on regular classroom teachers and special education teachers to become clinical teachers. Clinical teaching can be seen as the process of assessment, planning instruction, carrying out the instruction, evaluating student performance, and modifying the instructional plan based on student performance. By clinically analyzing the child's learning ecology, the teacher is able to design instruction appropriate for the unique needs of each child.

Teacher assessment is an integral component of individualizing instruction for educationally handicapped children, and it must be understood that assessment does not refer to looking exclusively within the child to discover the problem. Rather, assessment refers to that process of evaluating the child's total learning ecology to find not only the source of the academic problem but also the solution to that problem.

The educationally handicapped student's learning ecology includes the child's performance in school but also includes, among other things, the curriculum, the teaching methodology, the instructional materials being employed, and the home and neighborhood environment. Have the child's instructional objectives been properly sequenced? Has the child been effectively reinforced for on-task behavior? Is the child's home life supportive of homework or enrichment activities? These and other significant questions are important considerations in assessing the educationally handicapped child's total learning ecology, and they are crucial considerations in finding academic solutions for each child.

The sequence of the instruction that has been provided and is being provided to the educationally handicapped child is of vital importance. One of the major reasons for the importance of instructional sequence is that it is fundamental to the essential strategy of task analysis. If there is anything particularly special about special education, it is the use of task analysis in determining the specific curriculum to which the children should be exposed. Task analysis is the most important element in individualizing instruction because it targets the specific instructional gaps in an educationally handicapped student's academic performance history. The hierarchy or task ladder of sub-skills is the sequence of instructional objectives that should be included in an educationally handicapped child's individualized instructional plan.

In addition to individualizing the curriculum through the use of task analysis, a teacher of educationally handicapped children must primarily rely on direct instruction as a teaching strategy. Educationally handicapped children learn best when direct instruction from a teacher is provided, but equally importantly, direct instruction allows the teacher to profit from the plethora of assessment information that can be obtained from each child.

The process of assessment, planning, and teaching educationally handicapped children can be viewed as a form of continual environmental manipulation. By manipulating various aspects of the child's environment such as curriculum, instructional materials, or groupings, teachers can determine a child's pattern of strengths and weaknesses and whether particular teaching interventions are working. One of the major environmental manipulations with which teachers of the educationally handicapped must become proficient, is the management of the consequences of student behavior. When a student engages in appropriate behavior, such as increasing time on task, increasing the rate of learning, or raising a hand before talking, the teacher must learn to immediately provide the student with something the student likes or desires. Similarly, teachers must learn the difficult task of ignoring (and seeing that others ignore) inappropriate behavior.

Many individuals are interested in the school performance of educationally handicapped children. Most often these children are taught by a regular classroom teacher and a special education teacher. In addition, administrators, counselors, and specialists are also typically involved in the lives of educationally handicapped children. Certainly parents and primary care givers are not only very interested in the school performance of such children but are in an ideal position to contribute meaningful information to the teachers. Collaboration among these groups of people is critical to the ultimate success of the educationally handicapped child.

J.C.

ACKNOWLEDGMENTS

Sincere appreciation is expressed to the Mount Saint Mary's College class of 1964 whose generosity contributed significantly to this project.

I wish to express a debt of gratitude to the many colleagues and students with whom I've worked who have contributed to the points of view I have expressed herein.

I want to acknowledge with heartfelt thanks the contributions of Lisa Lima, Heather McCarthy, Tina Young and especially Tamara Hatch who provided invaluable assistance in manuscript preparation.

Most importantly, I wish to express sincere gratitude to Jackie Lynn Campbell, whose unconditional support over the years has been a source of strength and encouragement.

CONTENTS

INDIVIDUALIZING INSTRUCTION
FOR THE
EDUCATIONALLY HANDICAPPED

Chapter 1

WHO ARE THE EDUCATIONALLY HANDICAPPED?

Special education teachers are frequently faced with the responsibility of facilitating the learning of children who do not fit snugly into the major categories of special education. These children are typically educated for at least part of the day in Resource Rooms or by itinerant teachers. All special education teachers must develop teaching strategies that will enhance the opportunity for these children to improve their academic difficulties and increase the rate at which they learn. For those times that they are not in special education pull-out programs, these children are taught in the regular classroom. Consequently, regular classroom teachers must also develop efficient and effective strategies for teaching these children.

It would not be appropriate to refer to these children only as mentally retarded; however, many of them are indeed mentally retarded. It would similarly be inappropriate exclusively to use the term learning disabled or behavior disordered, but most certainly, some of these children have learning disabilities or behavior disorders.

What can be said is that all of these children have school related **handicaps**. The term handicap is deliberately chosen to distinguish it from disabilities. There are many with disabilities (the inability to perform a task) who are not handicapped by that fact. Jim Abbott, the former major league baseball pitcher, was not handicapped by the lack of a right arm, and Beethoven was not handicapped by his deafness. Most assuredly these two men were disabled. (Abbott couldn't salute the flag right-handed; Beethoven could not hear whispers.) However, it is fair to argue that they did not suffer handicaps (limitations placed on them by society) because of their disability. Handicaps can be seen as a limitation placed on someone because of that person's inability to perform. For this reason, a lack of success on school-related tasks can be viewed as a handicap.

The term, therefore, selected to describe children who do not fit neatly into a category, but who are either identified as requiring special education or who are woefully behind their age peers in some or all academic areas, is *educationally handicapped.* The term educationally handicapped is used to represent the children who exhibit mild forms of mental retardation, learning disabilities, and behavior disorders. These children have more characteristics in common than they have characteristics that place them in specific special education categories. Also, outside the classroom they are often indistinguishable from one another and from other children.

Every regular classroom also has children at the lower end of the distribution curve on a variety of variables. Depending on the variable, the students who represent the lower end of the distribution curve change. Educationally handicapped children often are near the lower end of the distribution on many variables and are most often mainstreamed or included to some degree into the regular education classes throughout the teaching day. Because more and more exceptional children are being integrated into the regular classrooms, special education teachers are being increasingly called upon to work collaboratively with the regular education staff to facilitate the learning of these children. Describing a program in rural Louisiana where mildly handicapped students were placed in regular education classes, Beckers and Carnes (1995) found that substantial academic and social progress was observed by the end of the school year, parental support had increased, and more general education teachers wanted to be involved in the inclusion program.

Educationally handicapped children can be identified as children who should receive special education services and will have an Individualized Education Plan (IEP). The special education teacher and the regular classroom teacher will unquestionably be called upon to participate in the development of that IEP and to execute some of that plan in the regular classroom. In addition to the identified exceptional children, there will be children who have not been identified as requiring special education services but who perform consistently and significantly below average. These children can be considered to be educationally handicapped as well.

Children with educational handicaps represent a variety of deviations from the norm. Some of these children have sensory problems such as hearing or visual impairments. Others may have physical or chronic health problems, but all will have learning or academic achievement problems of some kind. Who educationally handicapped children are is conceptualized in Figure 1.1.

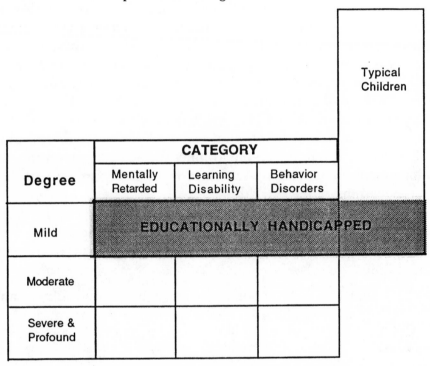

Figure 1.1 Who are the educationally handicapped?

What we have are children, who for any number of reasons, do not do well in school. For example, a student may not be successful because his tantruming behavior prevents him from attending to the learning task, or another student may "tune out" because she is withdrawn and introverted. Similarly, another student may be performing two or three years below grade level on an academic task while yet another may have difficulty because they have a below normal innate potential. On the one hand, we might say they are underachievers, slow, learning disabled, or mildly mentally retarded. On the other hand, we could say that they do not possess the necessary prerequisite skills to engage in the behaviors they are expected to perform in school. Clearly the latter is a better approach than the former because it leads to strategies of intervention. Regardless of the point of view a teacher adopts, the child is there in the class, with all his manifested characteristics, and the teacher is expected to facilitate his learning.

What can be said with confidence about these children is that each and every child is an individual with his or her own pattern of strengths and weaknesses. All of these children are experiencing academic underachievement, and the reasons for that underachievement are tied to their individuality. Many of these children have attention problems and exhibit a variety of different kinds of behavior problems within the classroom. Almost all of these children experience frustration and exhibit that frustration in a variety of ways. Another point that can be made with confidence is that all of these children respond to direct teaching. The literature is also clear (Kessissoglou & Farrell, 1995; Murphy, 1988) that an environment which provides immediate reinforcement for correct performance is an environment that facilitates the learning of these children.

ETIOLOGY OF EDUCATIONAL HANDICAPS

The problems of these children can be caused by an infinite number of variables. Some children are underachieving because of less innate potential than other children. Some have not developed appropriate adaptive behavior skills while others have been raised in an environment so malignant that normal learning has not occurred. Others come from environments which sustain patterns of behavior which are so dysfunctional that their learning is severely inhibited. It may even be that some of these children in fact have some type of mild neurological dysfunction, although that is always difficult to unequivocally pinpoint.

Innate Potential

Clearly some children do not have the innate potential to be as successful academically as typical children. Innate potential is often described as intelligence, and although intelligence has proven to be relatively unimportant in terms of teaching children, it is nonetheless a reasonable explanation of some children's inability to perform academically. The problem with intelligence is its elusiveness. On one hand people think of intelligence as innate potential, and yet on the other hand, the only reasonable measurement of intelligence that we have is IQ. Even though intelligence can be delimiting, it should not be thought of as predetermining a particular level of performance. The best way to think of intelligence is to think of it as the result of the interaction between heredity (nature) and the environment (nurture). That interaction is what produces the particular level of measured intelligence that we call IQ. Obviously, the more enriched the environment in which a child functions, the higher the IQ will be. One helpful mental image of intelligence is that of a rubber band. If you think of the rubber band as it lies on the table as the contribution of heredity or nature and the rubber band stretched between your fingers as the measured level of performance resulting from the individual interacting with the environment, you can easily understand the interaction of nature and nurture. Obviously, rubber bands come in different lengths (just as children are born with different innate potentials). It is equally true that rubber bands can be stretched to different lengths (the impact of nurture on measured intelligence).

Teachers have all occasionally made negative decisions regarding a child's potential based on a less than satisfactory IQ score. An IQ score of one or more standard deviations below the mean does not necessarily indicate a lack of innate potential. It is better to interpret this score as reflecting the child's present level of functioning without making forecasts of future performance. It is far better to consider intelligence as a measured level of performance than it is to consider it an indicant of innate potential.

Historically speaking, D.O. Hebb (1949) hypothesized a perfectly reasonable understanding of intelligence. Hebb called intelligence "A" the raw material with which we are born or in other words the innate potential. He called intelligence "B" measured intelligence or in other words that which IQ tests measure. It is imperative to understand that an IQ score is not an indication of innate potential but rather an individual's existing level of performance. Said another way, it is the rate at which an individual is currently learning. An IQ score must never be viewed as an indication that places a child in a certain academic role for the rest of his life. In point of fact, IQ can change (in either direction). That is to say, if one increases the rate at which a child learns his IQ will go up. Similarly, if one decreases the rate at which a child learns his IQ will go down.

Nature-Nurture Controversy

What is it that allows an individual to achieve a given level of intellectual performance (intelligence "B")? Is it the native intelligence he was born with (intelligence "A") or is it the degree of environmental favorableness within which he has interacted over a period of years? This is the classic heredity/environment or nature/nurture argument which has been going on for years.

The most common sense solution to this dilemma has been offered by Dobzhansky (1955) more than forty years ago. Dobzhansky maintained that every individual is born with a certain genotype (Hebb's intelligence "A"). He hypothesizes many genotypes, four of which are shown below:

Genotype A - Level of Innate Intelligence Commensurate
With Moderate Mental Retardation

Genotype B - Level of Innate Intelligence Commensurate
With Mild Mental Retardation

Genotype C - Level of Innate Intelligence Commensurate
With Normal Performance

Genotype D - Level of Innate Intelligence Commensurate
With Gifted Performance

However, it is crucial to understand that being born with a certain genotype does not guarantee that an individual will necessarily function at a particular intellectual level. If that were the case, heredity would account for all human performance.

Dobzhansky successfully accomplished an interactional posture between the heredity and environmental points of view. He suggested that each individual's genotypic intelligence is affected by the type of environment to which he is predominantly exposed. The degree to which this interaction takes place will determine what the individual's measured intelligence (Hebb's intelligence "B") will be.

An individual who had been born with Genotype C who was reared in a restricted non-stimulating environment could quite possibly have obtained a measured IQ of 65-75, while the same individual raised in an enriched stimulating environment could have achieved an IQ of 110-120. This range of possibilities of measured performance is what Dobzhansky called a *reaction range*. All of Dobzhansky's genotypes have reaction ranges with the less innate potential having smaller ranges than genotypes with more innate potential.

This concept of reaction range is extremely important to teachers of educationally handicapped children. It is certainly more advantageous for the teacher to assume that a child has not achieved his maximum level of performance and that by providing a rich, stimulating learning environment, the child will continue to improve academically.

Environmental Enrichment

Another factor which significantly affects children's learning is the degree of environmental favorableness in which they function. There is general agreement that the degree of environmental favorableness affects the academic performance of children who are mildly mentally retarded and children with mild behavior disorders. There is a growing sentiment (Case, Harris, and Graham, 1992; Englemann, Carnine, Johnson, and Meyers, 1989; Lloyd, 1988) that the same is true for children with learning disabilities. In fact, it is good to remember that all of these children share more characteristics in common than they do differences.

It is generally agreed that more than 75 percent of the children identified as mentally retarded are functioning at that level because of the conditions in the environment in which they were reared. Characteristics of a malignant environment include stark poverty, parental abandonment, cruelty and neglect, parental drunkenness, family drug abuse, continual rejection, malnutrition, cultural barrenness, caregiver's indifference to education, adverse child rearing practices, sensory deprivation and an absence of sensory stimulation during infancy. It is not surprising that children raised in such circumstances have educational handicaps.

Educationally handicapped children also represent children with mild learning disabilities. Learning disabilities, which are often manifested as difficulties in the acquisition and use of listening skills, speaking skills, reading, writing, and reasoning or mathematical abilities, are presumed to be due to a dysfunction in the central nervous system. Once again there is little value in debating whether central nervous system dysfunction actually exists or not. Manifested learning problems could also be attributed to the child's educational environment— i.e., poor teaching, improper sequencing of instruction, or inappropriate instructional materials. What is abundantly clear is that brain injury or cerebral dysfunction is extremely difficult to determine based on behavioral characteristics; and even if the existence of this problem could be categorically verified, it does nothing to suggest instructional strategies.

The one characteristic that must exist for a child to be identified as learning disabled is a manifested academic difficulty. The origin of the field of learning disabilities was the attempt to identify reasons why children were not performing successfully which could not be attributed to mental retardation, sensory impairments, or other existing categories. In addition to problems of academic achievement, teachers often see problems with hyperactivity, perceptual motor impairments, emotional highs and lows, as well as disorders of attention, impulsivity and problems with memory. These characteristics are remarkably similar to the characteristics of those who have been identified as mildly mentally retarded. Clearly, mildly mentally retarded children do not perform well academically. They have problems of emotional lability and exhibit below-normal motor skills. They also have serious problems with memory and attention.

Other educationally handicapped children are children with behavior disorders. These are sometimes referred to as emotional problems. Very often these behavior disorders are characterized as either a child turning inward to manifest certain characteristics or turning outward to express particular problems. Turning inward may be understood as children who are withdrawn from peers and who do not have adequate social relationships with peers or adults. Occasionally, some children will also exhibit signs of depression and delusions.

Outward kinds of problems tend to be described as excessive anger or hostility. Hyperactivity and emotional outbursts are other characteristics which have been observed in children with behavior disorders. Temper tantrums, various forms of preoccupation and unusual boredom and disinterest also characterize children with behavior disorders. Most certainly the panoply of manifested behaviors associated with behavior disorders are maintained or indeed strengthened, by a variety of elements in the child's environment. These children inevitably exhibit a lack of success in the classroom and do not perform academically as well as typical children.

THE EXCLUSION SYNDROME

There is an item on the 1972 Stanford-Binet Test of Intelligence which aptly summarizes what had happened to educationally handicapped children in many of our public schools.

> When there is a collision, the last car of the train is usually damaged most. So they have decided that it would be best if the last car is always removed before the train starts out. What is foolish about this statement? *

On the surface this statement does seem silly or foolish, but when we realize that children were being removed from regular classes and segregated in self-contained special education settings just like the last car is removed from the train, the situation becomes more serious. The intention in segregating children in special classes was to obtain two relatively homogeneous groupings, i.e., the special class and the regular class. Obviously however, this did not occur, and it was soon confirmed that heterogeneous groupings continued to exist in both classes. It is relatively impractical to attempt to eliminate individual differences. Not only is it impractical, but it is also essentially impossible. It is far better to treat each child as an individual and teach him or her according to his or her needs.

Fortunately, in our more recent history we have seen a movement away from excluding children and away from an attempt at homogeneous groupings; instead we are witnessing a commitment to keep children integrated into their regular classes as much as possible. Even so, some children (i.e., those identified as needing special education) will require individualized instruction and special education support services if they are to be effectively integrated into their regular classes.

---

*Stanford-Binet Test of Intelligence (1972) Verbal Absurdities IV-Year 11.

THE INEFFECTIVENESS OF LABELING

The children who are typically mainstreamed into regular education programs come from those populations of exceptional children known as the mildly mentally retarded, the learning disabled, and children with mild behavior disorders. These categories, sometimes with different names, have existed for many years. However, the categories in and of themselves offer little in terms of specific teaching suggestions or instructional strategies. In most special education textbooks, these categories are subdivided into mild, moderate, and severe and profound groupings. Generally speaking a child who is mainstreamed into, or included in, the regular classroom is the child who would fall into the mild subdivision.

MacMillan et al. (1996) point out that the mildly retarded are distinctively different from the more moderate and severe forms of mental retardation. Consequently they propose developing a new term that "captures the pervasive weakness in abstract reasoning and problem-solving" that the mildly retarded exhibit as opposed to "the 'general dysfunction' evident across contexts in moderate to profound forms" (357). They state that although Reschly (1988) suggested the term Educationally Handicapped, they are leaning more towards the term Generalized Learning Disability.

In looking at children who have been identified as mildly mentally retarded, mildly learning disabled and mildly behavior disordered, we find in many ways that the children are indistinguishable from one another. Similarly we find that they have many educational characteristics in common and most importantly the strategies for facilitating the learning of these children are not in any way category-specific, but rather are individual to the child. There is no reason that the same strategies of instruction which happen to be appropriate for mildly mentally retarded children would not be similarly appropriate for children with learning disabilities or a behavior disorder.

An assessment procedure which leads to labeling a child is a relatively inefficient procedure in terms of determining appropriate curriculum for that child. Arriving at a categorical label frequently becomes an end in itself, and unfortunately, explaining a student's behavior in terms of that categorical label becomes circular reasoning. For example:

A principal observing in Miss Jones' class sees a student engaging in the following behaviors:
- She cries frequently.
- She engages in frequent tantrums.
- She has poor academic performance.
- She is hyperactive.
- She often starts arguments.

Miss Jones describes how this student acts as emotional disturbance. Now the principal moves on to Miss Smith's class and observes another student engaging in similar behaviors to the student in Miss Jones' class. The principal, guilty of circular reasoning, says that this student is engaging in these behaviors **because** he is emotionally disturbed.

An arbitrary label, i.e., emotional disturbance, was attached to a set of behaviors; then similar behaviors on the part of another student were explained as that arbitrary label. All too frequently a label provides a justification for a teacher's or a school's inability to succeed with a student. This is not to say that there are not some children who need intensive, self-contained special education programs. However, the majority of educationally handicapped learners can be served in the regular class with resource room or other types of special education support. This is true regardless of the label or category which might be attached to a child. Hallahan and Kauffman (1997) explain that among children classified as educable mentally retarded, learning disabled and emotionally disturbed, there are more similarities than differences. In other words, the label does not lead to curricular or methodological strategies.

THE NEED FOR SPECIAL EDUCATION SUPPORT

Regular education frequently does not meet the needs of all children. The number of children currently receiving special education services is adequate testimony to that conclusion. There are over 5,370,000 children receiving special education in America's public schools as of 1993-94. This is an increase from slightly over 5,150,000 in 1992-93. In 1976-77 there were just over 3,700,000 children being served. The growth in the number of exceptional children being served is staggering. Today more than 71 percent of exceptional children are being served in a combination of resource rooms and the regular classroom. (U.S. Department of Education, 1995).

For years, special education was category specific. That is, programs were designed for mentally retarded children, for learning disabled children, for children with behavior disorders, for hearing impaired children and for virtually every other category that existed or came to exist. Although the intent in establishing these categories was to create homogeneity, the children sharing these labels proved to be a very heterogeneous group. Also the self-contained special classes established for these categories proved not to be efficacious academically. In other words, we have learned that there is no one way to teach a label.

Inter-individual differences are the basis of exceptionality and have resulted in the creation of categories and labels. For example, comparing children on individualized IQ tests and adaptive behavior scales has led to the use of the label "mentally retarded." However, intraindividual differences do not lead to labels but instead identify appropriate curriculum objectives. For example, two learning disabled children who are underachieving in Reading by three grade levels could be underachieving for very different reasons. The differences within each student will determine the individualized learning objectives for each student. Chapter 2 will consider this concept in more detail.

HOW ARE EDUCATIONALLY HANDICAPPED CHILDREN SERVED?

These children who represent the milder levels of mental retardation, learning disabilities and behavior disorders are most frequently served in a resource room and are mainstreamed into regular classes for a portion of the day. Reblin (1994) observed that language-learning disabled students in pull out programs were not generating skills which generalized to the regular classroom. In her study she found that such children benefitted in many ways from a new model where they were fully included in the regular class and were not pulled out for special instruction or services. In this model the resource room teacher and the speech/language therapist co-taught in the regular classroom with the regular classroom teacher for specified periods every day.

A resource room is a service delivery model in special education where the student spends a part of each day working with a special education teacher and special education support personnel outside the regular classroom. The child is integrated into the regular education classroom to the degree possible for that portion of the day that she is not in the resource room. Farmer and Farmer (1996) found that in a mainstream situation, students with exceptionalities were well integrated into their classroom's social structure. They conclude that concern that students with exceptionalities would be outcasts in mainstreamed classrooms was not supported by the results of their study. The amount of collaboration between the special education teacher and the regular education teacher is considerable. This is especially important because much of the student's IEP can in fact be carried out in the regular classroom by the regular classroom teacher. However, in order to maximize the child's learning opportunities, both the special education teacher and the regular education teacher need to develop strategies for individualizing instruction in both settings.

Another model somewhat less frequently employed is the itinerant teacher model. In this model , a special education teacher would come into the regular education classroom and work with those educationally handicapped children who have been identified and for whom IEPs existed. Sargent (1992) concluded that promoted students with special needs who were served by itinerant teachers, tended to perform better than those who were not promoted and were served in a special class. Typically, the number of visits from the itinerant teacher and the amount of time spent with a particular student is determined by the identified student's level of need.

Occasionally, school districts will employ consultant teachers whose responsibility is to work directly with the classroom teacher and not with individual students. Conducting a five-year study of learning disabled students in mainstreamed classes and resource room programs, Osborne et al. (1991) found that over the five years of the study special education and regular education teachers interacted with increasing frequency. They also found that teachers rated students who were mainstreamed higher on behavior related to academic competence. The advantage of this model is that the classroom teacher has an additional person with whom to discuss curricular and methodological strategies. The disadvantage of course is that there is not an additional teacher available to work directly with the educationally handicapped children.

These are the primary service delivery models which involve the regular classroom teacher. There are other models of course—typically used for more severe handicapping conditions such as self-contained special classes and special schools. However, perceived benefits of integrating even moderately and severely handicapped students in regular classes includes social benefits of developing friendships, feeling a part of a school and a classroom and increased levels of self-esteem (Janney et al., 1995).

THE CONCEPT OF MAINSTREAMING OR INCLUSION

At the present time and certainly in the future there can be little doubt about the need for both special teacher and regular teacher involvement in the teaching of educationally handicapped children. The integration of educationally handicapped children in the regular class is sometimes called mainstreaming and sometimes referred to as inclusion. In either case the Least Restrictive Environment (LRE) for these children, for at least a part of each school day, has been determined to be the regular classroom. Inclusion is not to be confused with the term "full inclusion" which implies the elimination of the concept of LRE and any placement options for handicapped children other than the regular classroom. Educationally handicapped children are currently mainstreamed into or included in regular classes and the frequency of that mainstreaming or inclusion is likely to increase in the years ahead.

Mainstreaming is a concept which originated with the development of the Education of All Handicapped Children Act (PL 94-142) in 1975. Under the rubric of the least restrictive environment children are mainstreamed into regular classes depending upon their ability to function in such an environment. It is the child's needs and not the type of services available that determine where on the continuum of services the child is placed. Clearly, the regular education classroom is a less restrictive environment than segregated special education settings.

There are basically three types of mainstreaming:
1. physical mainstreaming
2. social mainstreaming
3. academic mainstreaming

Physical mainstreaming simply means that special education students share a physical plant with nonexceptional children. In other words, they may have a self-contained class in the neighborhood school. Social mainstreaming means that special education children interact with nonexceptional children in settings such as the lunchroom, the playground and the assembly hall. There is social interaction but the special education children are not integrated into the regular classroom for academic instruction. Social interaction is not an insignificant objective. Merz and Merz (1992) found that the greater the degree of integration, the fewer the number of learning disabled students who manifested significant deficits in social competencies. Academic mainstreaming means that the special education children are integrated into the regular class to the degree possible for as much academic instruction as possible. It is academic mainstreaming which brings classroom teachers and special education teachers together as partners in developing academic programs for educationally handicapped children.

Discussing the integration of special needs students into vocational classes Greene et al. (1991) point out that the integration is greatly enhanced when vocational teachers and special needs personnel are able to employ four fundamental strategies:

1. Clinical Teaching which they describe as tailoring learning experiences to vocational students' needs (p.14).

2. Environmental/Curriculum Modification which involves adjusting or changing the classroom physical or instructional environment to accommodate the unique abilities, needs, learning styles, and occupational goals of special needs learners (p.14).

3. Direct Instruction which is characterized as an instructional strategy emphasizing direct roles for vocational teachers as opposed to the involvement of peer tutors or other instructional support systems (p.15).

4. Individualized Instruction which focuses teaching on individual learners. "Individualized instruction does not require that teachers work one-on-one with students. Rather, the method allows students to work at their own pace using a variety of instructional materials and resources to facilitate their learning" (p.15).

These strategies when applied to the elementary school curriculum are precisely the strategies special education teachers and regular education teachers need to employ in order for educationally handicapped children to be successful in school.

REFERENCES

Beckers, G.G., & Carnes, J.S. (1995). Proof positive–inclusion works. Paper presented at 73rd annual convention of the Council for Exceptional Children, Indianapolis, IN. ERIC# ED 385090.

Case, L.P., Harris, K.R., & Graham, S. (1992). Improving the mathematical problem-solving skills of students with learning disabilities. *Journal of Special Education, 26* (1), 1-19.

Cullinan, D., Sabornie, E., & Crossland, C.L. (1992). Social mainstreaming of mildly handicapped students. *The Elementary School Journal, 92* (3), 339-351.

Dobzhansky, T. (1955). *Evaluation, genetics, and man.* New York: John Wiley.

Englemann, S., Carnine, L., Johnson, G., & Meyers, L. (1989). *Corrective reading: Comprehension.* Chicago: Science Research Associates.

Farmer, T.W,. & Farmer, E.M.Z. (1996). Social relationships of students with exceptionalities in mainstreamed classrooms: Social networks and homophily. *Exceptional Children, 62* (5), 431-451.

Greene, G., Albright, L., Kokaska, C., & Beacham-Greene, C. (1991). Instructional strategies for students with special needs in integrated vocational education settings. *The Journal for Vocational Special Needs Education, 13* (2), 13-17.

Hallahan, D.P., & Kauffman, J.M. (1997). *Exceptional learners.* Boston: Allyn and Bacon.

Hebb, D.O. (1949). *The organization of behavior.* New York: John Wiley.

Janney, R.E., Snell, M.E., Beers, M.K., & Raynes, M. (1995). Integrating students with moderate and severe disabilities into general education classes. *Exceptional Children, 61* (5), 425-439.

Kessissoglou, S., & Farrell, P. (1995). Whatever happened to precision teaching? *British Journal of Special Education, 22* (2), 60-63.

Kirk, S.A. (1972, 1962). *Education of exceptional children.* Boston: Houghton Mifflin.

Lewis, A., Wilson, S.M., & McLoughlin, T.F., (1992). Resource room and the consulting model for servicing low achieving students: A review and analysis. *B.C. Journal of Special Education, 16* (3), 259-281.

Lloyd, J.W. (1988). Direct Academic Instructions in Learning Disabilities. In M.C. Wang, M.C. Reynolds, & H.J. Walberg (Eds.), *Handbook of special education: Research and practice, Vol. 2. Mildly Handicapped Conditions.* New York: Permagan Press.

MacMillan, D.L., Siperstein, G.N., & Gresham, F.M. (1996). A challenge to the viability of mild mental retardation as a diagnostic category. *Exceptional Children, 62* (4), 356-371.

Merz, K.W., & Merz, J.M., (1992). The effect of service delivery model on the social-behavioral competence of learning disabled students. *B.C. Journal of Special Education, 16* (1), 82-91.

Murphy, J. (1988). Contingency contracting in schools: A review. *Education and Treatment of Children, 11* (3), 257-269.

Osborne, S.S., Schulte, A.C., & McKinney, J.D. (1991). A longitudinal study of students with learning disabilities in mainstream and resource programs. *Exceptionality, 2,* 81-95.

Reblin, P.A. (1994). A first grade inclusion model that trains classroom teachers to modify and develop curriculum for language-learning disabled students. ED 374605, Ed.D. Practicum report Nova Southeastern U.

Reschly, D.J. (1988). Minority and mild retardation: Legal issues, research findings, and reform trends. In M.C. Wang, M.C. Reynolds, & H.J. Walberg (Eds.), *Handbook of special education: Research and practice, Vol. 2. Mildly Handicapped Conditions.* New York: Permagan Press.

Chapter 2

CLINICAL TEACHING

How does a teacher determine the teaching/learning experiences to which her educationally handicapped children should be exposed? What information does a teacher use to group children for instructional purposes? Clearly these are important questions, especially given that educationally handicapped children have been unsuccessful in the educational experiences to which they have heretofore been exposed. Consideration will be given to individual differences and the implications of those differences on the development of curriculum. A thorough examination will be given to the process of informal educational assessment and the teacher's role in that process.

Teachers are charged by their school districts or their state departments of education to teach a specific curriculum to particular grade levels of children. This is perfectly understandable and reasonable and provides a broad scope of education for the children in that district. Each teacher at each grade level in the district contributes to the broad scope of educational goals embraced by that district. Of course a major problem often arises if teachers simply attempt to follow curriculum guides or unit plans in "cookbook" fashion. More often than not in such cases, educationally handicapped children experience considerable difficulty. These children are often missing major pieces in the body of knowledge which are prerequisite to what they are being asked to learn, and consequently each year they tend to fall further and further behind.

As an alternative to simply following curriculum guides, teachers of educationally handicapped children should give serious consideration to addressing the variety of individual differences which these children manifest. In doing so, the teachers would not be disregarding the school district's curriculum guide or required educational goals, but rather subdividing those goals and breaking them down in an attempt to teach the educationally handicapped children the skills and knowledge which are missing in their behavioral repertoires. Only then will these children be able to proceed through the required curriculum.

In order to be certified for special education, many educationally handicapped children are labeled mentally retarded, learning disabled, or behavior disordered. The mere use of labels such as learning disabled or mildly mentally retarded can be costly to the student unless the teachers judiciously remember that these terms are only a general description of observed behavior and do not in any way explain the exhibited behavior or the problems these children are manifesting. Many children share labels or categories, but each of them is different on a host of school-related dimensions. However, we group children for academic purposes, heterogeneity exists to a much greater degree than homogeneity. Think how different each child is who is labeled normal. Each has his own particular pattern of strengths and weaknesses. The same thing is similarly true for educationally handicapped children. Each educationally handicapped child is functioning at his or her particular level for a variety of uniquely individual reasons. Even two children who are achieving at exactly the same level could be achieving at those levels for entirely different reasons. Said another way, each child has his or her own individual learning profile, and each child's program must be adapted to meet his or her particular needs.

IS THE PROBLEM IN THE CHILD OR IN THE LEARNING ECOLOGY?

We have already given cursory consideration to what intelligence is and the impact of the interaction between nature and nurture on that variable. We should remind ourselves that the only aspect of intelligence that we truly have to work with is measured intelligence or IQ. Because it is not a true indication of innate potential, it cannot adequately explain school performance in educationally handicapped children, and it cannot assist the teacher in matching the student with an appropriate instructional environment. Like labels or categories, intelligence can be used as a description of behavior but often falls considerably short when it is used as an explanation of behavior.

Many terms, like intelligence, are often inadvertently used as an explanation of a teacher's not being successful in facilitating the learning of educationally handicapped children. If a teacher convinces herself that a child doesn't have the "intelligence" to learn, it would not be surprising if the child experienced minimal or zero success. Additional terms which can provide built-in explanations or justifications for limited progress include terms like motivation and readiness. In order to be useful to the teacher, such terms must be operationally defined so that their meaning becomes tangible and observable. When they are so defined they can be useful descriptions of behavior exhibited by educationally handicapped students, and they will not be used as justifications for teachers not being successful.

GROUPING FOR INSTRUCTION

Individualizing instruction does not mean simply teaching each child on a one-to-one basis. Greene et al. (1991) has pointed out that individualized instruction does not necessarily require the teacher to work exclusively in a one-on-one situation with a student. Clearly appropriate groupings are possible and equally true is the fact that students can work at their own pace and with instructionally appropriate materials. Most assuredly children can be grouped for instructional purposes if they share the same instructional objectives. Grouping children for instructional purposes is a problem teachers have been pondering for many years, and no simple method of grouping seems to be completely effective. The best situation seems to be a variety of groupings depending upon the material being presented. It may be appropriate to group child A, child B and child C together for specific language instruction but have each of those children members of very different groups for instruction in subtraction. The inevitable individuality of educationally handicapped children (in fact all children) makes this type of grouping strategy not only desirable but in fact necessary if they are to be successful.

Every individual in the world is like every other individual in some ways. Similarly each individual manifests characteristics which make him or her entirely unlike any other individual in the world. This is most emphatically true for educationally handicapped children. For years educators have given lip service to the term **individualized instruction**; however, this is precisely the only way in which these children can be effectively taught. Specifically, the individual differences which educationally handicapped children manifest must be the precise basis for their individualized curriculum. These differences determine exactly what each child needs and consequently should be taught by the teacher. It must be remembered that the fact an individual is labeled behavior disordered or developmentally disabled in no way suggests that he can necessarily be taught in a similar fashion to other children who share those labels. The most important attitude for a teacher to have is that he or she is teaching children and not labels and that every child brings to the classroom his or her own particular pattern of strengths and weaknesses.

The essential element in successfully teaching educationally handicapped children is individualizing their instruction. Instruction is only meaningful for these children if it is designed to meet the individual needs that they manifest. Said another way, educationally handicapped children need to be evaluated in terms of their dependent versus independent behaviors. That is to say that there are some behaviors with which a child may need a tremendous amount of assistance while there are others with which he or she is relatively independent. One educationally handicapped youngster may be independent in terms of mathematics and yet be quite dependent in terms of reading. Another child may exhibit the exact opposite profile. The teacher's task could be expressed as attempting to maximize the number of independent behaviors in an educationally handicapped child's repertoire.

THE TEACHER'S ROLE

Sometimes the soundest pedagogical strategies were established early in the history of education. Just as the principles of instruction that Itard used with Victor in the 1700s are still appropriate as special education strategies today, Smith (1969) suggested some responsibilities of teachers who are working with mainstreamed or included learners. Those strategies can be summarized as follows:

1. Help students develop increasingly higher levels of competency in a variety of curricular domains.

2. Recognize that students differ dramatically regardless of any attempts at homogeneous grouping.

3. Because teachers have access to specific and frequent student performance data, teachers should be primarily responsible for gathering this data.

4. Teaching/learning strategies must be individually designed to meet the needs of individual students.

In order to effectively work with handicapped learners, teachers must perform constant educational assessments and build individual curricula based on that continuing assessment data. The importance of teacher assessment is highlighted by Shapiro and Ager (1992) when they state, "... a clear recognition exists of the need to make assessment more closely linked to the instructional practice (283)." The basis of teacher assessment is **student variability**. All children manifest individual differences or heterogeneity in their academic performance, and these are the variables upon which teachers develop individualized programs. Said another way, children's performances vary decidedly depending on the variable being considered. Two ten-year-old boys, Quentin and Wilbur, may both be labeled Learning Disabled. However, Quentin may be considerably more proficient in reading than Wilbur is, while Wilbur might be the best math student in the class. Obviously they need individually designed programs in order to realize their maximum potential. Teachers are in the best position to gather diagnostic and assessment data on children like Quentin and Wilbur because they have access to daily observations of the students' performance. We all know that reliability increases as the number of observations increase. Clearly then, a teacher's daily observation of student performance results in more reliable information than one-shot observations such as tests or interviews. It isn't that tests are not important, but the daily observations of the teacher are a much more reliable indication of the student's true performance. Teachers must accept the responsibility of determining what a student's needs are and for developing curriculum appropriate to those needs.

INDIVIDUAL DIFFERENCES

Individual differences were recognized by Itard, but it was Kirk (1962) who began using the term discrepancies in growth and later

(1972) the terms inter-individual variability and intraindividual variability. Ultimately, it was Smith (1968, 1974) who brought the importance of these concepts to the fore under the rubric of **clinical teaching**.

Perhaps an example might help to make the point more lucid. Admittedly the following example is not the type of problem typically encountered by special or elementary education teachers; however, it does serve the purpose of highlighting the point. Suppose we are interested in studying the foul shooting ability of a college basketball team. The coach has decided that foul shooting is a necessary skill a student should have in order to successfully survive in his environment. If we were to randomly sample a large enough group of college basketball players and chart their foul shooting ability, we would probably see that the distribution would fit what is commonly called the bell-shaped or normal curve.

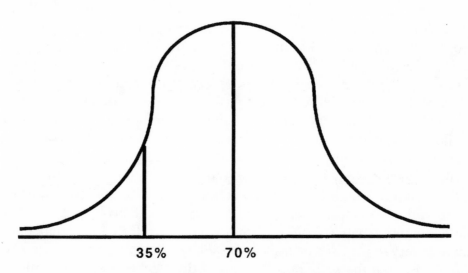

35%   70%

Figure 2.1 Percentage of successful foul shots.

In this hypothetical example the mean of our foul shooters is 70 percent. Notice that this is the high-point of the curve, and very few people could make 90 or 100 percent. Now let's look at two foul shooters who shot only 35 percent. We could say in effect that these were underachieving foul shooters. That is not too dissimilar from saying that two students who are ten years old who are reading at the first grade level are underachieving readers. We must be very cautious,

however, not to assume that because the two students are underachieving at the same level, that they are underachieving for the same
reason. In other words, we cannot assume that any one given remedial program will successfully remediate both students. What we need to
do is break the skill down into its component parts and evaluate each
student in terms of those component parts. Let's take a look at foul
shooting and select some components that might constitute a skill of
shooting foul shots. Let's assume that we can break foul shooting down
into leg strength, arm strength, eye sight, agility, and balance. Now we
can compare our two underachieving foul shooters on these component parts of foul shooting.

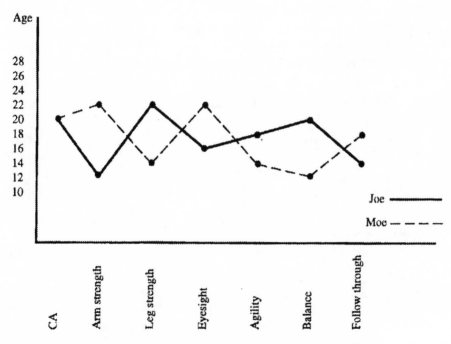

Figure 2.2. Individual variability of two foul shooters.

Notice that both boys are 20 years old and for the sake of argument let's say that they are identical twins who have been raised together in the exact same environment. However, when we begin to look at the components of foul shooting we begin to see that although the boys scored at exactly the same point, they show remarkable differences. Notice that Joe is particularly weak in arm strength and eye sight, whereas Moe's particular weaknesses seem to be leg strength, agility, and balance. This suggests that each boy needs a different and individual program of remediation if we are, in fact, going to remediate the reasons why he is not performing at a level commensurate with his peers in foul shooting. Joe needs a program emphasizing arm strength and eye sight development. Moe, on the other hand, needs a program designed to develop the strength of his legs, his agility, and balance. What do you suppose would happen if both boys were exposed to the same remedial program? It doesn't take too much investigation to see that one would profit and one would probably remain at the same level of achievement. Let's suppose that we exposed both boys to a program of remediation emphasizing arm strength and eye sight. Perhaps Moe is already performing at peak efficiency in these areas, so it is questionable as to how much benefit a remedial program of this nature would be to him. He would probably not profit to any great degree from this type of program. Whereas Joe, who is weak in these areas, would profit immensely. This in the author's judgement is the essence of individualizing instruction, and consequently must be the basis of curriculum decisions.

It becomes obvious after examining these data that the same remedial program would not serve both players equally well. A program emphasizing arm strength, agility and balance would be effective for one player but would essentially ignore the deficiencies in the other. The need for further elaboration on the necessity of **individualized** programs is hopefully unnecessary.

INTRAINDIVIDUAL VARIABILITY IN READING

Following the preceding noneducational example, a look at the diagnostic process in an educational example may be helpful.

Clinical teaching actually begins with a teacher recognizing that a child is experiencing some type of difficulty in class. Once this recognition is made, he or she will want to begin eliminating some possible causes of the student's dysfunction. For example, consideration should be given to serious visual problems, auditory problems, or speech problems. Assuming that none of these problems is present, a general achievement test should be given in order to establish an achievement profile. This service is often provided by school psychologists or curriculum specialists. The Peabody Individual Achievement Test is one of the achievement batteries often used for this purpose. Among other information this instrument provides age and grade equivalents in mathematics, reading recognition, reading comprehension, spelling and general information. The hypothetical profile of two students is depicted in Figure 2.3.

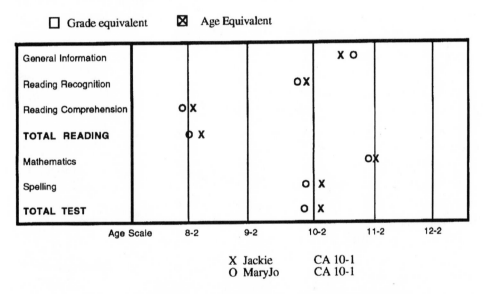

Figure 2.3 Age score profile of Jackie and MaryJo on PIAT-R

After examining the profile it is easy to see that the major weakness of both girls is reading comprehension. At this point it would be appropriate to administer a test such as the Woodcock Reading Mastery Tests. This instrument assesses letter identification, word identification, word attack, word comprehension and passage comprehension. It provides a more penetrating analysis of the concept of reading comprehension and is a test that often can be given by the classroom teacher.

Suppose that it has been determined that both girls are very weak in word identification and word attack. It is important to remember that this is still not enough information to design individual instructional programs for each of the girls. Figure 2.4 shows the major components of reading and Figure 2.5 a breakdown of the word recognition skill in the reading task hierarchy.

WORD RECOGNITION
MEANINGS
COMPREHENSION
STUDY SKILLS
FLUENCY AND RATE
INTEREST AND APPRECIATION

Figure 2.4 Components of reading.

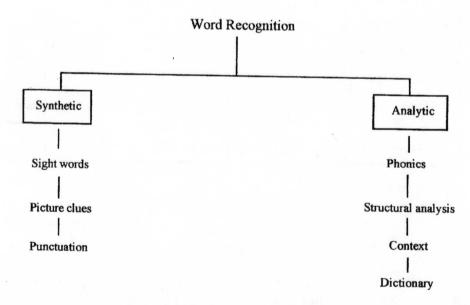

Figure 2.5 Word recognition breakdown.

One of the girls may have difficulty with phonetic analysis and further observation by the teacher reveals that she cannot make particular sound blends and has great difficulty with long vowel sounds and with final consonants. The other girl would be identified as having a problem with structural analysis. Her difficulty might be reading punctuation, not differentiating between prefixes and suffixes, or between singular and plural, or understanding contractions. Other students could have different kinds of problems that fall under the rubric of word recognition or word identification. One student can have problems with comprehension such as making inferences, identifying the main idea, or sequencing the events of the story. Other students could have difficulty with sight words or picture clues or other visual skills requiring discrimination and visual memory. The point is that information like this is precisely what is needed to develop an individualized curriculum for each student.

Let's look at another example in the area of reading—**meanings**. This could be defined as the use of prior experience and immediate context clues in the material to develop one's own understanding of what is being communicated. Some fundamental questions in this area a teacher might investigate to develop individualized curriculum could be:

1. Do the students expect to gain meaning from what they read?
2. Do students use a range of strategies such as skimming, scanning, or asking themselves questions as they read?
3. Do the students use context clues such as headings, subheadings, pictures, captions, and diagrams to help build meaning?
4. Do the students know how and when to use a dictionary?
5. Are the students able to link what they are reading to their previous experience?
6. Do the students have their own ideas or prejudices which interfere with their obtaining meaning from the text?
7. Are the students able to identify the main points or main ideas from a text?
8. Are the students able to follow the author's line of argument throughout the reading assignment?

Let's for example assume that it has been determined that a student does not effectively use headings, subheadings, pictures, captions, and diagrams to develop meaning. In such a case a teacher might give the students a reading assignment in a newspaper and have them read only the headings and captions and explain the photographs. She could ask the students to predict what the articles will contain, then ask them to compare their thoughts with the full text of the actual article.

She could give a student or small group of students a piece of reading text and ask them to discuss appropriate titles for it. She could also have the student look at a specific piece of text and ask him or her to identify the ways in which the writer helps the reader by providing information that guides the reader through the material.

Under the rubric of obtaining meaning, another student may have difficulty extracting the main points or main ideas from a text. Some ideas which may be helpful in this area would be to discuss with the students what they understand by a "main idea." The teacher could ask the student to tell her, or perhaps another student, what the text is about. She could say to the student "Imagine that your friend has been absent from school and has missed the first part of the story. What would you tell him to help him understand the rest of the story that he is going to read?" Another idea would be to offer the student a piece of reading text and a number of statements, some of which are main ideas. The teacher could ask the student or pairs of students to decide which of the statements are in fact main ideas. Students in pairs or small groups could be asked to read a series of paragraphs and create a title for each paragraph.

Good teachers are more than capable of coming up with a host of similar ideas to attack various weaknesses that students will manifest not only in the area of reading but in all curricular areas. Specific teaching ideas for reading and mathematics will be covered in detail in Chapters 7 and 8.

CLINICAL TEACHING PROCESS

In order for teachers to be successful at individualizing instruction they must become proficient clinical teachers. The clinical teaching process was originally conceptualized by Smith (1968) and has been adapted for summary in Table 2.1.

The teacher's task really begins at Level Four when he or she is called upon to perform a task analysis on the areas of the curriculum in which the educationally handicapped student is being unsuccessful and continues through Level Five where individual education plans (IEP) are developed with the proper collaboration for each individual student.

Table 2.1 *Clinical Teaching Process*

| Level 1 | Screen for gross, obvious problems, Eg.: speech impediments, visual/hearing impairments, serious emotional/behavioral problems. Refer to appropriate specialist. |

| Level 2 | General Achievement Tests to confirm or determine the existence of problems in learning. Review and analyze profile of each child |

| Level 3 | Administration of Diagnostic Tests to determine the relative strengths and weaknesses each child manifests on the major components of each academic area. |

| Level 4 | Task analysis and informal, teacher-made assessment activities to develop individual, specific academic and non-academic targets. Also a look for possible environmental correlates of manifested difficulties |

| Level 5 | Developmental of Individualized Education Plan in consultation with appropriate support personnel followed by placement of child in most appropriate settings. |

There are a variety of teacher assessment models available to special educators and regular classroom teachers. After looking at all the curriculum-based assessment models, Shapiro and Ager (1992) suggest that the models be integrated. They go on to emphasize that such a practice "would require the joint efforts of general and special education teachers and other related educational personnel—(284)." In discussing teacher competencies in the area of assessment, Walker and Bruno (1993) state, "The master teacher should be able to organize assessment information into an appropriate IEP and use information gathered by all team members to adjust methods and material for specific students" (p. 14).

Task analysis and collaboration are covered in subsequent chapters of this text. For now suffice it to say that the keys to teaching the educationally handicapped are **individualizing instruction** and **task analysis**. An important aspect to carrying out this teaching/learning process is collaboration with others involved in the education of the particular child.

Instructional programming or deciding what to teach an educationally handicapped child depends upon assessment of each child's strengths and weaknesses. Hopefully it has been established that assessment is an ongoing part of the teaching process and by looking at the clinical teaching model (Fig. 2.6), we can see that assessment includes formal tests—both achievement and diagnostic, observation, and informal assessment techniques which are basically teacher-made and are always part of the regular instructional activities. The following types of activities can easily be adapted for informal teacher assessment:

1. seatwork
2. orally administered exercises
3. individual written assignments
4. supervised small group work.

Assessment, including informal teacher assessment, must never be an end in itself and must always be designed to lead to instruction. It may be nice to know that Mioki is reading at grade level 1.2, but isn't it much more useful to know that Mioki knows the names of all the letters but only the sounds for "a" and "m" ?

ESSENCE OF TEACHER ASSESSMENT

What we are really talking about is the whole basis of educational diagnosis. Diagnosis is based on the concept of variability. There is the kind of variability that exists between individuals. If it weren't for this kind of variability there would be no basis for exceptionality. If we didn't compare one child with another child and say, for example that Charlie has a lower IQ than Dorothy, or Don is reading two grades below Audrey, there would be no basis for exceptionality. The other kind of variability is the variability that exists within each one of us. This is the kind of variability that was hopefully pointed out by showing the comparison of Joe and Moe and their ability to shoot foul shots or Jackie and MaryJo and their ability to read.

Of all the professionals who interact with students the teacher is in the most advantageous position to gather diagnostic information. A shrewd and competent teacher will be able to gather necessary information and from it develop pertinent remedial strategies. Below are some general suggestions as to how teachers should go about this necessary task.

1. Every diagnostic activity should be part of the ongoing program.

2. Try and make activities interesting to the student, i.e., you are attempting to obtain maximum performance. Activities should be varied.

3. Activities should be selected to directly measure specific educational dimensions. For example, phonic blends, math facts, visual memory, and auditory discrimination.

4. Activities should directly measure the child's performance, for example, if you are interested in a youngster's ability to interact with adults, provide him with the opportunity for this kind of activity.

5. Evaluate frequently and attempt to obtain maximum performance.

Above all, teachers should remember that the most productive thing they can do is to look for the problem and its solution in the learning ecology and not within the student. This type of educational assessment will lead most directly to a strategy of intervention and will help teachers become successful clinical teachers.

"Assessment, however, must be viewed as only part of a total process which includes implementing interventions derived from that assessment as well as measuring their outcomes. Instruction needs to relate constantly to assessment, and, likewise, assessment should be the basis of intervention" (Shapiro & Ager, 1992).

REFERENCES

Greene, S., Albright, L., Kokaska, C., & Beacham-Greene, C. (1991). Instructional strategies for students with special needs in integrated vocational education settings. *The Journal for Vocational Special Needs Education, 13* (2), 13-17.

Kirk, S. A. (1979, 1962). *Educating exceptional children.* Boston: Houghton Mifflin.

Polloway, E.A., & Patton, J.R. (1993). *Strategies for teaching learners with special needs.* New York: MacMillan Publishing Co., Ch. 3 "Strategies to Develop and Maintain Individualized Programs," 29-54.

Shapiro, E.S., & Ager, C. (1992). Assessment of special education students in regular education programs: Linking assessment to instruction. *The Elementary School Journal, 92* (3), 283-296.

Smith (1974, 1968). *Clinical Teaching: Methods of Instruction for the Retarded.* New York: McGraw-Hill.

Smith (1969). *Teacher Diagnosis of Educational Difficulties,* Columbus, OH: Merrill.

Walker, S.C., & Bruno, R.M. (1993). Defining assessment and diagnostic competencies for master level special education teachers. Paper presented at Annual Convention of the Council for Exceptional Children, San Antonio, Texas. April 5-9, 1993. ERIC# ED 364009.

Chapter 3

TEACHER ASSESSMENT OF THE
LEARNING ECOLOGY

Hopefully the inappropriateness of looking exclusively within the child to determine the reasons for academic under-achievement and other unsatisfactory school performance has been sufficiently established. The child's overall environment or the **learner's ecology** should be completely examined in an attempt to determine the causes of and solutions to the learner's inadequate or inappropriate performance. A careful analysis of the total environment in which the educationally handicapped child functions will inevitably yield clues to successful remediation. This type of assessment is an ongoing part of the instructional process, and the students performance data will document whether the objectives formulated from the assessment are appropriate and are being met. In a report to the New Zealand Ministry of Education on teacher assessment, Wiley and Smith (1992) state, "Most of the assessment practices were closely linked to the curriculum emphasis and classroom organization of the schools, and were mainly used to diagnose children's individual needs to guide teaching effort, and to group children to provide them with appropriate learning resources" (p. 7).

WHAT IS THE LEARNER ECOLOGY?

The learner ecology can include the student's performance on academic tasks, the student's behavior on tasks other than academic activities, and teacher variables such as instructional activities, curriculum, and instructional materials. For example, is a student's lack of success on an educational objective indicative of the need to break the task in question down into component parts and create a new objective targeting a prerequisite skill? Is the student's deportment conflicting with his being on task? Is the sequence of the curriculum logical; are the instructional activities appropriate to the learner's objectives; and are the instructional materials the best choices for the particular learning activities?

The setting is also part of the learner ecology. For example, what type of physical environment exists in the classroom? This includes the arrangement of the desks, the degree of lighting, the temperature, and the degree of comfort in interacting with the teacher. Sometimes a teacher's expectation of an educationally handicapped child's performance can be a delimiting factor in student performance. Sprouse and Webb (1994), discussing the influence of the Pygmalion Effect on spelling and essay tests, state, "There is strong evidence for a Pygmalion Effect in grading which needs to be considered by teachers" (p. 21-22). The learner ecology also includes social interactions. For example, what are the types of groupings in which the student is involved? Is the student comfortable with any peers that might share the same classroom? Is the student comfortable with the teachers and the aides? Is the student free from fear and anxiety? "The ecology of human development is the scientific study of the progressive mutual accommodation, throughout the life span, between a growing human organism and the changing immediate environments in which it lives, and this process is affected by relations obtaining within and between these immediate settings..." (Brofenbrenner, 1977, 514). This suggests in the strongest possible terms that all of a child's environments have an impact on his or her development. The classroom is a microsystem in the child's ecology. Brofenbrenner indicates that a microsystem is made up of the multitude of relations between the child and an immediate setting containing that child—such as the classroom.

There are additional factors that should be considered when looking at the learner's ecology. "Ecological experiments must take into account aspects of the physical environment as possible indirect influences on social processes taking place within the setting..." (Brofenbrenner, 1977, 523). For example, the learners' life circumstances are important. Does the student come from poverty? Is there drunkenness or abuse in the family? Is the child homeless? Or are there other problems which could be of such magnitude to prevent his concentrating in any meaningful way on learning tasks? It would be well to know if there had been any significant traumas in the child's developmental history. An example of these traumas could be losing a significant amount of hearing, or vision. Were there any significant diseases encountered by the child such as meningitis which could have a debilitating impact on his learning?

In assessing an educationally handicapped child, another fundamental question to ask is "To what extent is the student's problem the result of inadequate teaching?" All of these issues are important because each and every one could possibly affect student performance on important educational tasks.

TYPES OF ASSESSMENT

Before getting too deeply into the concept of teacher assessment of the learner ecology, it is appropriate to give cursory consideration to the general concept of assessment. Assessment in its broadest sense has several purposes, and it is often conducted by a variety of individuals. Generally speaking, there are five types of assessment (Salvia & Ysseldyke, 1995):

1. Referral of students
2. Screening of students
3. Classification of students
4. Instructional planning for students
5. Student progress evaluation

The most important type of assessment to the teacher is assessment for instructional planning. Assessment done by others including assessment done by school psychologists or curriculum specialists seldom ever provides specific direction in terms of what to teach a particular child. Even though the broader scope of curriculum is often prescribed by the particular school district, it most frequently falls to the teacher to create lessons built around the individual objectives for each child. This is particularly true for educationally handicapped children who for any number of reasons have fallen behind or who are not performing consistent with the general expectations of the group.

TEACHER ASSESSMENT

The classroom teacher or the special education teacher is clearly in the best position to conduct meaningful assessment activities relative to the child. The most important reason why teachers are in an ideal position is that they have the most *reliable* observations of the student. Almost everyone else sees the child far less frequently than the teacher and often in contrived situations. Another important reason is *rapport.* No one else in the school setting is in a better position to have established positive rapport with the learner than the teacher.

It is commonly understood that testing is a part of assessment but is not synonymous with assessment. Assessment is the process of collecting data for the purpose of specifying problems and making decisions relative to student performance. Typically, assessment is concerned with three distinct types of problems.

1. **Academic problems:** These are the most common reasons for referral by classroom teachers. A teacher or a parent believes that the student is not performing at the level he is expected to perform in content areas such as reading, mathematics, spelling, social studies, and science.

2. **Behavior problems:** Students are often referred for psychological or educational assessment because they exhibit behavior which is inconsistent with the expectations of the teacher. Examples would be disruptive behavior, failure to comply, social interaction problems with peers, or excessive withdrawal.

3. **Physical problems:** Such as the inability to function in the learning environment for any number of physical reasons.

These problems are of primary concern to the classroom teacher and special education teacher because it will inevitably fall to them to make the necessary ecological modifications to facilitate a student's improvement in these areas.

Suggestions for Teacher Assessment Activities

In developing teacher assessment activities, the classroom teacher or resource room teacher should strive to:

1. Not create contrived situations—the more the assessment situation resembles the normal teaching activities, the more the student is likely to emit maximum performance.

2. Maintain assessment activities as a regular part of the instructional activities. As far as the student is concerned the teacher's assessment activities should be indistinguishable from the on-going instructional activities.

3. Directly observe the target skill. If you are interested in observing the child's ability to regroup from the tens column, measure that skill directly and avoid making inferences about it from other forms of behavior.

4. Attempt to avoid excessive familiarity. Collect assessment data regularly, but vary the tasks so that the child does not become overly familiar with the activities. One way to maximize the validity of the assessment activity is to keep the child from becoming so familiar with it that it no longer assesses the child's ability on the particular task.

5. Keep all assessment activities interesting. The more interesting the activities, the more involved is the student. An involved student is likely to emit his or her maximum performance on the task.

Assessment activities by the teacher can take many forms and are not and should not be overly sophisticated. Examples of activities which can be used for teacher assessment are:

1. Observations. Simply observe the child engaging in the target behavior.

2. Seatwork analysis. A tremendous amount of information is provided in the worksheets and other seatwork activities to which children are normally exposed. In other words, the instructional program should be designed to reveal assessment data.

3. Individual oral responses. A student making individual oral responses one-on-one to the teacher will provide a tremendous amount of diagnostic information. Any assessment activity should assess a specific task.

4. Oral responses in groups.

5. Error analysis in homework, seatwork, and class projects.

6. Routine quizzes.

Generally speaking the process unfolds as follows:

1. Once you have targeted an issue, obtain the student's current level of performance (i.e., establish the baseline).

2. Choose your diagnostic teaching activities.

3. Decide what aspects of the learner's ecology need to be modified.
4. Systematically make the modifications and continue collecting student performance data (A more detailed consideration of this topic is provided in Chapter 6).
5. Continually evaluate student performance data to determine if and what additional modifications to the ecology are required.

Assessment Terminology

Teacher assessment can be referred to in a variety of ways and by a variety of terms. Most of these terms fall under the general rubric of performance assessment. Performance assessment is often called authentic assessment, curriculum based assessment, or informal educational diagnosis. In general all of these terms refer to the teacher assessing specifically the student's performance on the tasks they are expected to perform in school.

Curriculum-based assessment like all performance based assessments requires that the curriculum or other aspects of the learning ecology be analyzed including the student's performance on tasks so that specific behavioral objectives can be formulated. Concern about where the student is to be placed follows only after a decision has been made about the learning activities in which the student should be involved.

TEACHER AS ENVIRONMENTAL MANIPULATOR

One of the many things a teacher is, is a manipulator of the environment. The teacher manipulates the environment by placing a student in a desk at the front of the row, by providing or withholding reinforcement after a behavior occurs, by deciding to change a student's short term objective, or by using a video tape as part of the teaching lesson in a particular subject.

Care should be exercised not to view the environmental manipulation as a mechanistic or pejorative activity. As a teacher tries activities, materials or groupings, she is continually manipulating the environment to the educationally handicapped student's advantage. By manipulating the environment, the teacher is able to continue the things that are effective and discard those that are not. Maybe by changing the environment from including the Harcourt Brace Series to one that includes the DISTAR Program that teacher facilitates the child meeting her objective in Reading. Maybe by using flash cards rather than work sheets a particular student will be successful in multiplication facts. One student's environment might be enhanced by the teacher including reinforcement in the form of social praise and smiling, while another student might respond better if his environment included reinforcement in the form of points or tokens.

Teachers can also assess the effectiveness of one-on-one instruction with the student in a resource room versus instructing that student in a small group in a resource room. Another strategy would be to assess the student's performance in the regular classroom in a situation that is guaranteed to eliminate the possibility of failure, as opposed to a situation in which the student might possibly respond incorrectly.

Example

Let's suppose that there are two students in the fourth grade who are having difficulty with multiplication problems that require two digits to be multiplied by two digits. On a recent mathematics achievement test, it was determined that both of these youngsters are performing at the third grade one month level in mathematics. A true clinical teacher would recognize immediately that these two children may not be underachieving for the same reason. Further analysis conducted simply as a part of the ongoing teaching/learning activity reveals that Zane has effectively memorized his multiplication facts but consistently makes errors when regrouping from the units column to the tens column or from the tens column to the hundreds column. Ashley, on the other hand, has demonstrated no difficulty with basic addition, and successfully regroups virtually one hundred percent of the time. Her problem is that she has not mastered the multiplication facts. Whereas Zane consistently multiplies 9 times 3 correctly, Ashley consistently makes an error when asked to perform that task. Ashley, on the other hand, can successfully carry to the tens column, but Zane consistently makes an error on this particular task. In order to successfully multiply two digit numbers by two digit numbers, Ashley needs coaching and practice with multiplication facts. She would prosper with flash cards, peer tutoring, and a consistent schedule of reinforcement for multiplication facts correctly answered. Zane, on the other hand, needs to be working on skills which are prerequisite to multiplication. He needs to be carefully instructed in simple addition and especially addition which requires regrouping and a complete mastering of place value. It is relatively easy to see how two distinct lesson plans and sets of objectives for these two children would be necessary.

A similar example in reading can be provided. Two fifth grade students are underachieving at approximately the same level in the area of reading. By identifying the tasks necessary to be successful at reading at the fifth grade level and having a sense of their proper sequence, the teacher is able to engage the two children in activities which will reveal their individual deficiencies. For example, Steve is a fluent reader, and seldom makes an error of phonetic analysis. He seems quite confident at reading new or unfamiliar words and has a good deal of confidence in his oral reading ability. However, after Steve has finished reading a passage, he frequently makes many errors on comprehension questions and cannot explain in his own words what he has just read. The teacher discovers that Steve simply does not know the meanings of the words he has read. Amber, on the other hand, knows the meanings of many words and seems to fully understand the story which has been read to her. Her problem is that she does not attack words phonetically with any degree of confidence and her inability to make sound blends and to smoothly read the words severely inhibits her ability to finish reading a passage in a prescribed period of time.

Abouzerd et al. (1994) in discussing teacher assessment of reading point out "–thoughtful teachers can, through assessment, pinpoint children's present theories about how words work and then design instruction using word sorts, word hunts, and other variations of word study that encourage children to achieve–" (p. 12).

This information could be obtained in a variety of simple in class activities, such as: (1) oral reading to the students and asking them questions, (2) asking the children to read out loud for one or two minutes to the teacher and then respond to questions from the teacher (3) timing the students while reading a passage silently, (4) informal short vocabulary checks and, (5) sound blending drills.

THE ASSESSMENT PROCESS

Basically the process of evaluating the learner's ecology follows the process depicted in Figure 3.1.

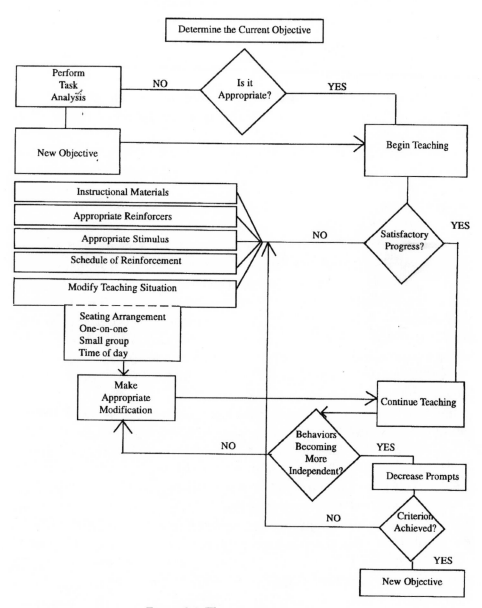

Figure 3.1. The assessment process.

The teacher begins by taking a critical look at the objective the learner is expected to meet. Does it appear to be an appropriate learning expectation based on what is known about the student's repertoire of prerequisite skills and individual pattern of strengths and weaknesses? If it does, it is appropriate to begin teaching. If not, the teacher must perform a task analysis to determine a more appropriate prerequisite objective. This process will be addressed more specifically in Chapter 4. As a result of the task analysis, a new objective is specified and the teaching process is begun.

Once the teaching/learning process begins to unfold, the issue of the learner's progress must be continually assessed. In other words, is the learner making satisfactory progress or not? If the answer is yes, the teaching/learning process is continued with regular checks and assessments of student progress and independence. However, if the answer is no, there are many factors of the learner ecology which must be assessed to determine what aspects of that ecology are contributing to the student's unsatisfactory progress.

Are the instructional materials appropriate? Unfortunately, little help is available in this area for the regular classroom teacher or the special education teacher. The motivation and consequences important to the publisher of educational and instructional materials is not necessarily the same as it would be for teachers or other special education personnel. Similarly, materials purchased by a school district are not purchased with a particular student's learning objectives in mind. Therefore, it falls to the teacher(s) to make the best decision possible in terms of the instructional materials. The guiding question should be "Are these materials that I am using with the student consistent with meeting the objectives that I have for that student?"

Are the instructional strategies and teacher prompts appropriate for the learning situation? Does the teacher need to reconsider the particular lessons she is using to help facilitate the learner's particular objectives. Are the prompts the teacher is using the most appropriate available? For example, instead of reading from a book, would it be better for the student if the teacher used flash cards?

Is enough time being devoted to the student achieving criterion? It is important to emphasize that with educationally handicapped children, accuracy is much more important than speed. This is not to say that increasing the rate with which a student performs particular educational tasks is unimportant; it is rather that accuracy is more important. Make certain that the student has enough time to achieve mastery and to completely learn the material.

Are the times of instruction the most advantageous that can be arranged? For example, if the student seems overly tired when exposed to a particular lesson in the afternoon, the teacher should ask himself/herself if it would be possible to provide that lesson in the morning. Similarly, questions could be asked about whether particular lessons would be more advantageous to students just before or just after lunch or just before or just after recess.

Are the types of settings in which the learner is expected to function the most appropriate? For example, is the objective expected to be met in the resource room or in the regular classroom or is the objective expected to be demonstrated in both settings? Will criterion be achieved in a one-on-one situation with the teacher or in small group instruction? Will the material be presented in small group or large group instruction? Will the learning be supported by cooperative learning activities or peer tutoring?

Are the social arrangements as satisfactory as can be arranged? In other words, does the educationally handicapped student have an opportunity to function with those he/she considers friends? Is the educationally handicapped student protected from bullies or others who would attempt to antagonize? If the teacher's aide has a particularly strong relationship with this student, is that aide given an opportunity to interact with the student and help him/her achieve criterion?

Are the consequences and reinforcers being provided appropriate to the situation? Are the consequences indeed reinforcing to the student or are they simply presumed to be reinforcing by the teacher? One of the best ways to determine whether consequences are preferred by the learner is to simply ask the learner. Finally in a related matter, one needs to ask whether the correct schedule of reinforcement is being used. If a behavior of importance was established using a fixed ratio of one or a continuous schedule of reinforcement, has an attempt been made to stretch that schedule of reinforcement so that the possibility of satiation can be prevented.

Once these issues have been addressed and all appropriate modifications made, the teaching activities are resumed. The next question in the assessment sequence is to determine if the learner's target behavior (e.g., reading rate, math accuracy, passage comprehension) are becoming more independent. In other words, is the learner achieving the success criterion with decreasing amounts of direct teacher attention? If not, all the aspects of the learner ecology should be examined and any necessary adjustments made. The overall goal is to assist the learner developing and maintaining competence in target areas.

All of these "diagnostic" activities can and should be done by the teacher in an ongoing fashion. They should be performed by the teacher because the teacher's daily interaction could lead to the opportunity for more consistency (reliability) in the observations than those obtained by specialists or support personnel and because social dynamics (rapport) is better between student and teacher than between student and any other member of the school's educational team.

These activities can be performed by the teacher if they are made as much a part as possible of the ongoing teaching/learning interaction. The approach suggested by Shapiro and Ager (1992) is to answer four questions related to academic skills.

1. To what degree does the instructional environment support successful academic performance? This question attempts to assess the relationship of the instructional environment to student performance. The importance of assessing the environment cannot be overstated.

2. To what degree is there a match between the student's instructional level (based on rate of performance) and the grade level material in which the student is currently placed? In general, this step of the process is conducted to determine if currently assigned grade level materials is matched to the student's instructional level.

3. What rates of acquisition and mastery are possible if presentation of curriculum is carefully controlled so the student always remains within instructional levels (based on accuracy of performance rather than rate) when learning new material.

4. The fourth and final step of assessing academic skills involves evaluating the outcomes of the intervention strategies. In other words, what is the extent to which the intervention strategies are successfully moving the student toward his long term goals in the curriculum. If an attempt is not made to separate assessment from teaching, the teacher would be able to blend the activities and obtain meaningful information which will facilitate students' success.

The main point to remember is that the place to look for explanations for poor student performance is not within the student. Even if there are internal explanations (e.g., low innate potential, neurological dysfunction), there isn't anything the teacher can do about it. The teacher should make a penetrating analysis of the learner's ecology, and most likely modifications can be made to significantly improve the learner's performance.

REFERENCES

Abouzerd, M. P. et al. (1994). Word sort: An alternative to phonics, spelling, and vocabulary. ERIC # ED 380774.

Brofenbrenner, U. (1977). Toward an experimental ecology of human development. *American Psychologist, 32*, 513-531.

Salvia, J., & Ysseldyke, J.E. (1995). *Assessment* (6th Edition). Boston: Houghton Mifflin.

Shapiro, E.S., & Ager, C. (1992). Assessment of special education students in regu lar educations programs: Linking assessment to instruction. *The Elementary School Journal, 92* (3), 283-296.

Spronse, J.L., & Webb, J.E. (1994). The pygmalion effect and its influence on the grading and gender assignment on spelling and essay assessments. Unpublished report. Curry School of Education. University of Virginia. ERIC # ED374O96.

Wyley, C., & Smith, L. (1992). Assessment and reporting practices in the first three years of school. Interim Report to the Ministry of Education New Zealand Council for Educational Research.

Chapter 4

SEQUENCING, TASK ANALYSIS, DIRECT TEACHING

SEQUENCING INSTRUCTION

How is the order in which content and skills are presented to educationally handicapped learners determined? Some would say it is determined by school district curriculum committees; some would claim local boards of education make the decision; while yet others might claim that the decision is really made by the publishers of textbooks and instructional materials.

Is the order or sequence of curriculum important? If teachers believe that education is a series of carefully planned, albeit interesting, but nonetheless disconnected units, the sequence of instruction might not seem important. On the other hand, if learning is seen as being dependent upon the mastery of prerequisite skills and knowledge, the sequence of instruction becomes critically important.

The importance of the issue is magnified for educationally handicapped learners because of the multitude of reasons in their learning ecology which contribute to their academic underachievement. Obviously if these children have gaps in their learning which constitute the prerequisite skills or knowledge for what they are being expected to learn, it will be difficult if not impossible to facilitate their meeting their objectives.

Curriculum Sequencing

Learning does not occur haphazardly, and it is a serious error to assume that it does not make any difference as to the order in which learning is presented to educationally handicapped students. In order

51

to be an effective clinical teacher, it is essential that a teacher develop a knowledge and a mind-set about the sequence in which instruction should take place. This is certainly not to suggest that there is only one proper sequence of instruction. As a matter of fact, the exact sequence of instructional activities is less important than the concept of proceeding in a sequential fashion. It is important that teachers develop a "plan of attack" for assisting the educationally handicapped child in accomplishing the educational objectives. Such a plan or sequence is provided in Nunan's (1989) book on the communicative classroom which addresses the sequencing and integration of tasks to formulate specific lessons.

An example not in the field of education may hopefully provide a metaphor skeleton on which the flesh and blood concept of sequencing instruction can develop. If you find yourself in New York City deciding to take a vacation to San Francisco, there are some crucial decisions which must be made. For example, you must decide on a mode of transportation. You could fly, take a bus, book passage on a train, or drive your car. You might choose flying because it is the fastest method, or you might elect a train because you have had considerable experience with trains. Let's suppose that you ultimately decide that the most sensible thing to do is to drive your car because it is the mode of travel which is best designed to help you accomplish your objectives. This would be similar to your selecting the Sullivan Reading series to help you meet the objective of reading with a particular student. It would not be appropriate to select alternative materials because they are easier for you to work with or because you are more familiar with them.

Once you have decided to drive to San Francisco, you must select the most propitious route. Suppose you decide to follow a route which takes you directly from New York to San Francisco. You would necessarily have to go through Ohio before you arrived in Indiana. Similarly, you could not get to Nevada without going through Utah. Hopefully the analogy with reading is again clear. You would have to determine your short term objectives and sequence them in the proper hierarchy. Because competency at any level is dependent upon competency in prerequisite skills, it would not be possible to omit objective four. Likewise, it would not be possible to accomplish objective eight before mastering objective seven. Each short term objective must be continually broken down into its component parts until the child is able to demonstrate competency.

The scope of instruction for many educationally handicapped children includes a consideration of readiness skills, academic instruction,vocational preparation, and social development.

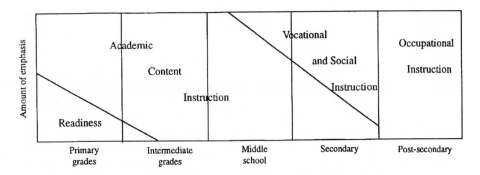

Figure 4.1. Sequential scope of curricular emphasis for
educationally handicapped students.

It is important to note that what might be a readiness skill for some objective could be an academic skill in another situation. For example, adding correctly is unquestionably a prerequisite skill to successfully mastering multiplication. However, for a different student, adding could be an academic objective in and of itself and there would naturally be other prerequisites to that objective.

Conceptually a student would enter a particular phase of academic instruction with entry level skills and would conclude that phase of instruction having achieved exit level skills. In an ideally sequenced educational program, the exit level skills of one aspect of the program become the entry level skills of the next. One of the primary if not the fundamental reasons that the need for special education exists, is because children have been exposed to an improperly sequenced instructional program and because there are gaps in their learning which prevent them from succeeding at the particular objectives to which they are exposed.

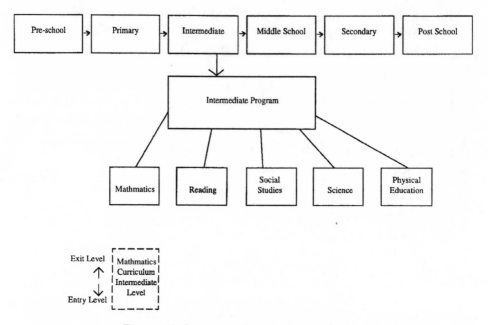

Figure 4.2. Sequence of curricular emphasis.

Instructional Sequencing

Most of the discussion thus far has focused on the acquisition of basic knowledge and fundamental comprehension. There is another type of hierarchy that may well come into play in the planning of instruction for educationally handicapped children. Benjamin Bloom's (1956) taxonomy of cognitive goals is not a sequence of learning objectives, but rather a hierarchy going from the less complex to the more complex. One does not have to possess all the knowledge he will ever need in order to engage in activities of comprehension or application. Similarly, complete mastery of application is not a prerequisite for any objectives focusing on analysis.

Bloom's Taxonomy of Cognitive Goals:
1. Knowledge–Knowing and remembering facts.
Example: The capital of Nevada is Carson City.

2. Comprehension–The ability to use knowledge.
Example: Explain the consequences of unemployment.

3. Application–The ability to use knowledge in a specific situation. Example: A student finding a particular article by using the ERIC database.

4. Analysis–The ability to break knowledge down into its component parts and distinguish among them.
Example: Write a critique of Milton Friedman's economic theory as it applies to employment.

5. Synthesis–The ability to create something new by combining old or existing knowledge.
Example: Explain learning by combining the ideas of Piaget, Erickson, and Bruner.

6. Evaluation–The ability to judge how well ideas, materials, or methods meet criteria.
Example: A speech on the impact of communism on the lives of citizens

Nevertheless, objectives focusing on application are more complex for the learner than objectives focusing on knowledge or comprehension. Simply because a child has an IEP or a special education label is not a reason to limit his learning objectives to knowledge of facts or basic comprehension. Educationally handicapped children, for whom their performance data suggest it is appropriate, could well have objectives which focus on application and in some cases analysis.

For example it may take an educationally handicapped child years to master the definition and recognition of a metaphor. At some point however, perhaps in middle school or high school, it may well be appropriate to expect the child to apply the skill by writing his own metaphors. Another example from social studies could focus on the topic of slavery. At the application level a child could be asked to "teach" the class or "illustrate" the necessary conditions for slavery to exist. At the analysis level he could be asked to compare slavery with indentured servitude.

The sequence, such as it exists, is the progressive increase in complexity as one moves from knowledge to analysis.

In addition to learning, sequence also impacts the manner in which a lesson is presented to a student. The sequence of instructional events has been identified and discussed thoroughly (Gagne & Briggs, 1992; Slavin, 1991; and Hunter, 1982.

In summary, the sequence of these instructional or teaching events are:

1. Obtain the learner's attention.
2. Review the material if necessary.
3. Provide a clear, precise new objective.
4. Present material and model the appropriate response.
5. Provide supervised practice.
6. Provide regular feedback.
7. Engage in periodic probes for learner understanding, comprehension, or mastery.

By attending to the sequence of instructional events, a teacher can maximize a particular student's opportunity to achieve competency on a host of instructional objectives.

TASK ANALYSIS

In addition to having a concept of the proper sequence of instruction, an essential skill for developing curriculum for educationally handicapped students is the knowledge and understanding of **task analysis**. Norton (1993) states that task analysis provides "...a more detailed answer to what should be taught regarding each of the selected tasks. Task analysis involves systematically breaking down each task, first into the steps that make it up...(p.4)"

Task analysis can be defined as identifying the component parts of the task and arranging them in sequential order. In writing his name, a student would have to know the letters before he could print the letters of his name. Before he could know the letters, he would have to be able to discriminate among shapes. Similarly, he would have to be able to write a straight line before he could write a particular letter. Before a straight line could be drawn the pencil would have to be properly gripped. As you can readily see, task analysis can be as fine or gross as you want it to be. It is not so important to have the exactly right sequence of tasks as it is to have an understanding of the importance of sequencing sub tasks to ultimately achieve success on the main task. An example of the task analysis of writing a name follows:

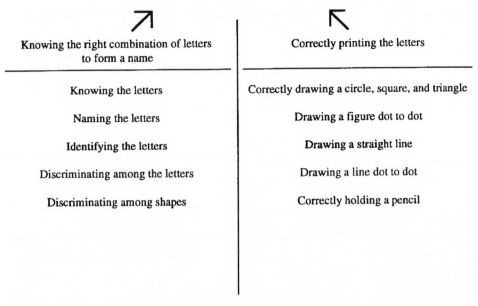

Knowing the right combination of letters to form a name	Correctly printing the letters
Knowing the letters	Correctly drawing a circle, square, and triangle
Naming the letters	Drawing a figure dot to dot
Identifying the letters	Drawing a straight line
Discriminating among the letters	Drawing a line dot to dot
Discriminating among shapes	Correctly holding a pencil

Figure 4.3. Task analysis of writing a name.

The teacher's job would be to determine where in the sequence a child fits and then to create specific objectives with a particular sub task (s). Next, lessons and activities must be designed to help facilitate the child's learning, and criteria must be established to indicate when it is time to move on to the next sub task in the hierarchy.

Unfortunately there is not a great deal of help available to teachers in the area of task analysis. Indeed some curriculum guides are organized in a logical sequence, but many of the objectives in such curriculum guides need to be broken down into sub tasks for educationally handicapped students. Consequently the strategies of task analysis are left to the teacher's judgment and analytical skills. Berdine and Cegelka (1980) stipulate "... task analysis refers to the procedure of carrying out these steps:

1. Identify a specific goal or objective.

2. Analyze that instructional objective into its component parts (i.e. the movements, actions, or responses that, when taken cumulatively, constitute the instructional objective).

3. Determine the entry level of the skill and specify the prerequisite skills (in other words, state at what point the particular skill sequence begins)." (p. 160)

The process of performing a task analysis can easily be seen in the following example from the academic content area of mathematics.

$$1.\ 6 + 3 =$$
$$2.\ 5 + 2 =$$
$$3.\ 1 + 7 =$$
$$4.\ 4 + 4 =$$
$$5.\ 3 + 4 =$$

A task analysis of these problems is depicted in Table 4.1.

Table 4.1. Task Analysis of Problems 1-5

Instructional Objective	Add with 80% accuracy problems containing two single-digit numbers whose sum is a single-digit number.
Sequence of Sub Skills	Uses vertical lines or x's and plus signs to write problems from numerals; counts total lines or marks to obtain answer.
	Counts two groups of lines or marks which are joined by a plus sign
	Reads a number problem with lines or marks. e.g. xxx + xxxx =
	Says plus when presented with written +
	Makes correct number of lines or marks indicated by single digit numeral
	Correctly counts vertical lines or marks
	Correctly counts manipulatives to 9
	Orally counts correctly from 1 to 9
Prerequisite Skills	Writes a + sign Makes lines or marks with pencil Holds pencil correctly Responds to verbal prompts

This strategy is predicated on the theory of learning being dependent on prerequisite skills. It does not require and in fact stands in opposition to the notion that a child has to be labeled before he can be helped or that the lack of success on an academic task is a problem within the child. Clearly one of the most important aspects of the child's learning ecology is the sequence of the instructional program to which he or she is exposed. It is essential to understand and embrace the concept of every child learning at a different rate and children possessing different degrees of the necessary prerequisite skills.

If Leslie and Kyle are first graders who cannot write their names, it would be a fundamental error to assume that the reason for not being able to write their names is the same for each child. An even more egregious outcome of that assumption would be the belief that both children could be taught or remediated in the same way. Leslie might not know the names of any of the letters and Kyle may know them all. Leslie may be skilled in using a pencil while Kyle may have difficulty even drawing basic shapes. Clearly the reasons for the two children not being able to write their names could be quite different. Once we have drawn that conclusion, it is relatively easy to conclude that each child requires an individual set of strategies to remediate the situation.

DIRECT TEACHING

How often have we heard expressions like "teach the concept," "understand multiplication," "appreciate sound blends," or "principles of spelling"? Surely the elusive nature of such terms can readily be seen. Any teacher who attempts to use terms like these in developing a teaching activity or creating a learning objective for a particular student will quickly see that these terms mean different things to different people. It is a much more effective and an altogether better strategy not to use these terms in forming objectives for students. It is better to use terms that specify what the student is expected to do. In using such specific or behavioral terms, it is much easier for the teacher to know when he or she has been successful and it is considerably easier for the student because he or she knows precisely what is expected.

Rather than teach Josh to appreciate sound blends, it would be better to teach Josh to correctly pronounce the "sh" blend nine out of ten times. Rather than teach Adam to understand multiplication, it would be better to teach Adam to correctly multiply all single digit numbers through nine.

The situation could be summarized as follows: If the child cannot do something that you consider to be essential for him to move forward in the learning program, teach the child to directly perform that task. Specify what you want the child to do and teach him or her directly to do that task. This simply means to teach a skill directly and not to assume that a skill will be transferred from some other type of activity. If students are having difficulty with word meanings, teach word meanings directly and do not, for example, assume that students will improve their ability at words meanings by participating in fluency activities. "The term direct instruction is used to describe lessons in which the teacher transmits information directly to students, structuring class time to reach a clearly defined set of objectives as efficiently as possible (Slavin, 1997, p. 23)."

Carnine (1981) suggests that there are four broad interrelated areas which constitute the components of **direct instruction**. These areas are: curriculum analysis, teacher training procedures, organization and development interventions for bringing about change in schools, and teacher presentation techniques. In examining teacher presentation techniques, Carnine (1981) maintained that a functional relationship exists between student performance and the teacher presentation techniques of rapid pacing, frequent praise, clear and precise signals, and consistent immediate corrections of incorrect responses. Carnine (1981) confirmed the value and benefits of direct instruction in his study of preschoolers using a multielement design. In this study he alternated high implementation and low implementation of these four teacher presentation techniques. For the first seven days of the study, he alternated the two implementation strategies daily and for the next twelve days he alternated them every third day. The two treatment conditions are summarized in Table 4.2.

Table 4.2. *Summary of implementation strategies of teacher presentation techniques*

Strategy	Implementation Level	
	High	Low
Pacing	Quick, lively, such as on "Sesame Street." Rapid fire teacher questions. (However, student answers are not rushed.)	Slow, dragged out. Inserted non-essential talk, longer pauses between questions.
Praise	Verbally recognizing a child's or group's response. Saying "great job," "boy, you're smart today," etc.	Zero or negligible verbal praise.
Signals	Clear. A visual or auditory stimulus that enabled students to answer simultaneously.	No explicit signals were given.
Corrections	Teacher immediately pointed out the error and repeated the task until all responded correctly.	Mistakes were ignored.

Carnine (1981) concludes that high implementation was clearly superior to low implementation. The high implementation strategy resulted in 95.5 percent correct answers (15% higher than low implementation) and an 85.1 percent on-task rate (compared to 50.6% for the low implementation group).

In addition to trying to implement these high implementation strategies, always make sure the child is absolutely aware of what is expected of her. The following principles are sound strategies to employ while teaching educationally handicapped children, and there is general agreement among educators that these steps characterize effective direct instruction.

1. State learning objectives and orient students to the lesson. Be sure they know what you will be teaching and what will be expected of them.
2. Review prerequisites. Make sure students have the prerequisites for the lesson.
3. Present new material. Teach the lesson that has been prepared using appropriate instructional materials.
4. Conduct learning probes. Ask questions to determine if the students are mastering the material.
5. Provide independent practice. Provide students with an opportunity to practice what they are learning.
6. Assess performances and provide feedback. Review seat work, give quizzes, have discussions. Let students know how their responses measure up.
7. Provide distributed practice and review. Spread the students' practice of their new skills over time and review their work regularly. (Slavin, 1997, p. 232)

In addition, teachers should endeavor to make their lessons and classroom activities interesting and stimulating and make every effort to keep the educationally handicapped child actively involved and participating in the teaching/learning activities. Finally, as is always the case when establishing new learning, provide immediate reinforcement for successful performance. According to Slavin (1997), direct instruction is especially appropriate when teaching a defined body of knowledge or specific skills. A good example of a direct teaching activity is provided by Constantino (1991). She developed a learning activity for at-risk students which focused on their decoding the consonants B, D, T, and S. The particular learning activities she developed were built around task analysis and specific objectives which were directly incorporated into the instructional activities.

Of course, once a task has been directly taught by the teacher, the objectives can and should be supplemented with what are sometimes thought of as indirect teaching strategies, such as seat work, readings, peer tutoring and cooperative learning activities. Even these activities, however, should directly address the expected target behavior for the student and should avoid conceptual leaps, assumptions and the need for the student to draw inferences.

Because few educationally handicapped students spontaneously generate and employ thinking and learning strategies, these strategies should be specifically taught as well. They should be practiced and built into the student's behavioral repertoire. One straightforward approach to helping educationally handicapped students learn to use such strategies calls for a direct instruction approach which includes teachers making the purpose of the strategy clear to the students; demonstrating the use of the strategy; providing coaching, practice opportunities, and regular feedback, and requiring students to think about how and why they use a strategy.

Outcomes-oriented teachers identify their students' behavioral objectives, select appropriate teaching strategies related to the target behaviors, and teach those strategies explicitly. There are a variety of academic strategies which have proven beneficial to many students, but educators have come to realize that most educationally handicapped students will not be successful without specific instruction on the identified tasks.

REFERENCES

Berdine, W.H. & Cegelka, P.T. (1980). *Teaching the trainable retarded.* Columbus: Charles E. Merrill.

Bloom, B. (ed.) (1956). *Taxonomy of educational objectives: The classification of educational goals.* New York: D. McKay.

Carnine, D.W. (1981). High and low implementation of direct instruction teaching techniques. *Education and Treatment of Children, 4* (1), 43-51.

Constantino, C. (1991). A learning activity for at risk first grade students in the decoding of consonants B, D, T, and S. ERIC #ED341034.

Gagne, R., & Briggs, L. (1992). *Principles of instructional design.* New York: Holt, Rinehart & Winston.

Hunter, M. (1982). *Mastery teaching.* El Segundo, CA: Instructional Dynamics.

Norton, R.E. (1993). Improving training quality by avoiding the "what errors" of curriculum errors. Paper presented at DACUM Invitational Seminar at the American Vocational Association Convention, Nashville, TN.

Nunan, D. (1989). *Designing tasks for the communicative classroom.* New York: Cambridge University Press.

Slavin, R.E. (1997). *Educational psychology.* (5th ed.). Boston: Allan Bacon. Chapter 5: The Effective Lesson.

Slavin, R. (1991). Are cooperative learning and untracking harmful to the gifted? *Educational Leadership, 48,* 68-71.

Smith, R.M. (1974, 1968). *Clinical Teaching:* Methods of Instruction for the Retarded, New York: McGraw Hill.

Chapter 5

INSTRUCTIONAL METHODOLOGY

Whereas curriculum can often be defined as the answer to the question of "What do I want the student to do?", methodology can often be understood as "How do I get them to do it?". Because a lesson plan is not the same as a recipe, teaching must not be seen as following a recipe in a cookbook. There are a multitude of unique individual situations a teacher will face when attempting to facilitate various aspects of learning in an educationally handicapped student. For this reason, it is important for a teacher to attach himself or herself to a theoretical underpinning from which any and all unique problems can be attacked. Another way of considering what a theoretical under-pinning is would be to consider it as a body of empirical evidence. The strongest body of empirical evidence concerning the facilitation of student learning, especially educationally handicapped student learning, appears to lie in applied behavior analysis.

If we understand that what we are expecting of the educationally handicapped child is for him or her to engage in some behavior, it becomes easier to use applied behavior analysis. If in fact what we expect of a student is not a particular behavior, it becomes quite difficult to determine whether or not we have been successful. More importantly it makes it impossible for the student to know if he or she has succeeded. To give further credibility to the applied behavior analysis school of thought, it is necessary for us to consider part of our job as teachers as that of manipulating the environment in such a way as to increase the frequency and duration of appropriate behaviors. Although we don't often think of what we do as teachers as being environmental manipulation, that is precisely what it is. We arrange the groupings of children, the stories to be read, and the activities to be engaged in. We provide the consequences of their behaviors or we allow the environment to provide those consequences. All of these activities are appropriate – they are part of what's called teaching, and they are forms of **environmental manipulation**.

For some children, the simplest, most straightforward methodology works best. Before making a learning task any more complicated than it needs to be, simply show the child what to do and ask her to do it. This of course assumes that you have broken the task down into some component parts and have identified an appropriate objective in that hierarchy. Sometimes children learn by simply being shown a task and being asked to perform that task. Similarly, children learn effectively by watching another child being taught a skill. A younger brother watches his father teach his older brother how to hit a baseball, and before long the younger brother is practicing the skill correctly.

OBSERVATIONAL LEARNING

People learn by watching others. Little brothers often watch big brothers in the backyard shooting a basketball at a basket. It is not an infrequent occurrence for the little brother to pick up the ball and try to emulate the big brother by attempting to shoot the basketball at the basket. Idiosyncratic fashions are also an example of this phenomenon. A multitude of teenage boys recently copied the fashion of wearing their trousers as low on their hips as possible. The examples from school are also legion. The chemistry teacher says to his students gathered around the work station, "Watch carefully as I pour this acid from the test tube into the compound in the beaker. It must be poured slowly and you must avoid inhaling the fumes." The students then duplicate this activity.

Observational learning looks at this process and examines the variables that influence its effectiveness. Albert Bandura (1977), a prominent behavioral psychologist, pioneered the work in observational learning. He became concerned that the behaviorists were not paying attention to the effects of students watching and thinking about the actions of others. In this regard Bandura's work provides a type of bridge between the strict behavioral approach which is extremely effective in many situations where the student's level of behavior is significantly below that of the other children and the more cognitive approaches to learning.

Observational learning occurs in two forms:
1. modeling
2. vicarious conditioning

Modeling Behavior

Modeling refers to changes in individuals that result from observing the actions of others. An educationally handicapped student watches her teacher explain and demonstrate how to perform short division procedures. As a result she is able to perform short division problems on her own. Sometimes a student can simply observe a classmate and profit from that observation. For example, an educationally handicapped student may observe his friend's approach to studying and preparing for an examination. As a result the educationally handicapped student may be able to incorporate those strategies and profit from them as well (Espin & Deno, 1989).

Modeling helps explain a powerful influence of culture on students' learning (Burgess et al., 1970). Parents are urged to set a good example and to avoid the "do as I say and not as I do" style of parenting. For example, parents are urged to use correct grammar when talking to their infants and young children, to engage in appropriate courtesy when interacting with children, and to demonstrate the family values which they consider important in their daily living.

One type of modeling is called **direct modeling**. This is a situation in which the learner simply attempts to imitate the behavior of another person that he wishes to model. For example, the educationally handicapped student who imitates his friend's studying behavior or a primary grade student imitating the way in which his mother prints the letters of the alphabet.

Symbolic modeling refers to imitating behaviors displayed by characters on television, in the movies, and in books. We have all seen children, especially teenagers, attempt to model the dress of characters on popular television shows. Obvious examples of this are duck tail haircuts among teenagers of the 1950s, bell-bottom pants and tie-dyed shirts worn by young people in the 1960s, the leisure suits of the 1970s and the return to pleated trousers in the 1980s.

Synthesized modeling means developing behaviors by combining portions of observed acts. For example, a young child may take a kitchen chair and climb up on it to reach a cookie jar and obtain a cookie after seeing her brother use that chair to climb up and reach a box of cereal on the shelf.

Finally, **abstract modeling** refers to inferring a system of rules by observing examples where the rules are displayed. Children frequently learn by inference the order of adjectives and nouns in English sentences by observing examples of those sentences. Sometimes children are taught these rules directly, but often the children seem to know the rules before they are specifically taught.

Vicarious Learning

While merely observing the actions of other people can affect the learner, the effects can be amplified if we also observe the consequences of those actions. This is known as vicarious learning or vicarious conditioning. This occurs when we observe the consequences of another person's behavior and adjust our own behavior accordingly. If an educationally handicapped student hears a teacher say to another student, "I really like the way you are working so quietly, Peter" or "I can tell how hard you studied for this spelling test, Dawn, because you did so very well," he is likely to be positively influenced by those compliments. Vicarious conditioning can also produce vicarious reprimands. If a student receives a verbal reprimand for leaving his seat, other students are also vicariously reprimanded for that action.

Learning a new behavior can be described as learning that did not exist prior to observing a model. For example, a youngster may never have successfully regrouped from the 10's column in a subtraction problem, but observing a fellow student engage in that activity establishes that behavior for the one who has been doing the observing. Another example would be learning how to factor a trinomial the first time a student observes her algebra teacher performing that function. Facilitating existing behaviors is also enhanced by the process of modeling. Observing how another student engages in studying behavior may help a particular student improve his own studying behavior.

Model Effectiveness

Two factors help to determine the effectiveness of a model for a particular student. The first factor is the similarity of the model to the student in question. This is why it is often better to have other students model appropriate behavior rather than just the teacher. Clearly other students are seen by educationally handicapped children as more similar to themselves than teachers are. The second factor is the perceived competence of the model. This is why it is often beneficial to use students who are recognized as being outstanding or superior students as models.

THE PROCESS OF OBSERVATIONAL LEARNING

Observational learning or modeling actually begins when the learners attention is attracted. Students are likely to pay attention when, for example, a fourth grade teacher expresses her view about fairness or when a high school social studies teacher talks about the significance of racial equality. In order for a student to profit from observational learning, the student's attention must be directed to the learning activity. But attention is not sufficient in and of itself. The learner's attention must be drawn to the critical aspects of the modeled behavior. For example, an English teacher trying to teach students to write clear expository paragraphs will probably not be successful by merely showing students well-written paragraphs. The teacher will have to direct the students' attention to the critical aspects of well-written paragraphs such as good introductory sentences, strong supporting statements, and a clear summary.

Once a student's attention has been focused on the critical aspects of modeled behavior, those aspects and those skills must be transferred to the student's memory. This involves mentally and physically practicing the task in a variety of ways. After some types of controlled practice, the students are usually prepared to practice the modeled behaviors individually, at first perhaps under the guidance of the teacher but later entirely on their own. This is where shrewd teachers will make use of seat work, practice activities and ultimately determine the success by employing quizzes or probes of some type.

MOTIVATION

It is also important to note that motivation is significantly influenced through observational learning. Motivation actually begins through direct or vicarious reinforcement. Students tend to engage in behaviors they have observed in others that result in reinforcement. Often the environment itself provides that reinforcement in addition to whatever reinforcers the teacher is employing. When a teacher praises a student for good work, other students are vicariously reinforced, resulting in motivation to continue working. In terms of behaviors which are reinforced by others, one merely needs to observe a continually changing pattern of teenage dressing habits.

In summary, it is often possible to simply call the educationally handicapped student's attention to a task; focus the student's attention to the critical elements of that task, and demonstrate the task for the student. If the student is able to successfully perform that task the behavior in question has been successfully modeled. Continued practice and assessment probes will continue to determine whether or not the behavior is becoming firmly established or whether it needs to be broken down into more discreet component parts.

BEHAVIOR MODIFICATION

Sometimes educationally handicapped children emit levels of performance which are so low in some areas that a more specific focus and series of objectives are required. In such cases, discrete behaviors need to be identified and appropriate objectives developed. When a teacher is faced with a situation like this, modeling and vicarious learning are most likely not appropriate and a more specific and direct methodology is called for. Behavior modification is arguably the most effective and efficient strategy to employ. Frequently referred to as precision teaching, consequence management, or behavior contracting, a teacher's use of behavior modification in the classroom falls under the general rubric of applied behavior management.

It's important to understand that behavior modification does not just deal with deportment or conduct; it deals with every form of behavior that children may emit in the classroom, from sitting in their

seats to solving arithmetic problems. Before delving into a consideration of behavior modification, however, it is helpful to consider one of
the fundamental learning models that you've no doubt encountered in
previous courses or texts. This model, called the Information
Processing Model, is a model which explains how children learn. It is
certainly not the only model, but it's one that provides a fundamental
explanation of the learning process. The input section of the model is
exactly how children receive information. As we all know, children
either hear information; they see it, or they touch it. Students some-
how receive information that goes into their brain and into their thinking process. The brain then processes the information; it's stored in
memory; it may be used, and then some form of output or response
occurs and that response serves as feedback and another form of input.

Focus will be addressed to the output section of the model and suggestions offered as to how and why it is important. All teachers have a
variety of objectives for their children. We want them to learn; we
want them to know things. But one of the fundamental points teachers
should think about is the question, "How do you know they have
learned something?" The only way you will know that a child has
learned something is by the child's responding in some way. They
must say something, write something, or do something in order for the
teacher to reliably draw the conclusion that they have learned. And
that is precisely where behavior modification comes in. The ability of
the teacher to increase behavioral responses, to maintain them, or in
the case of negative behaviors, decrease them, is fundamental to the
success of children's learning, especially the learning of educationally
handicapped children.

WHAT IS BEHAVIOR?

Before we can demonstrate an understanding of behavior modification, we must carefully consider what behavior really is. Many people
tend to think that behavior modification deals exclusively with deportment or conduct. This is not so; actually, it deals with all aspects of
human behavior. It includes anything an individual does which can be
observed by others. Behavior modifiers are indeed interested in
behaviors such as seat leaving or hitting one's classmates; however, it

should also be noted that behavior modification deals with academic behaviors such as reading, writing, and problem solving. It is important to remember that these too are behaviors which can be seen and counted and consequently managed by an effective system of behavior management.

Behavior modification is an effective and efficient system of managing all aspects of student behavior (Strandy et al., 1979; Luiselli & Downing, 1980). For behavior modification to be effective, however, it is imperative that teachers concern themselves with specific behaviors and not with nebulous, unverifiable assumptions. For example, the statement "Tina understands multiplication" is an assumption because understanding is a nebulous term which has different meanings to different individuals. However, this can be made more specific by stating this assumption in terms of an observable behavior by saying, "Tina writes the answers with 90 percent accuracy to a multiplication test." This is a behavior that can be seen, counted, and therefore managed. Even if a teacher chose to concern himself with a term like understanding multiplication, the student would necessarily have to behave or perform in some fashion in order for the teacher to make a decision that he does indeed understand multiplication.

Assumptions can be made behavioral by operationally defining what is intended. For example, the statement that Juanita appreciates music is an assumption made by someone who observes Juanita. We can operationalize this by saying appreciation of music will be defined as Juanita playing one of her classical music CDs at least two times a day as compared with a previous frequency of zero times a day. This operational definition removes the guesswork and no longer requires an arbitrary decision as to whether a criterion has been met.

The important thing to remember is that behavior modification deals with all aspects of student behavior and anything that a student does is behavior. Teachers must exercise every caution not to attempt to deal with assumptions, interpretations and other nonverifiable feelings. What one individual might interpret as an appreciation of music or understanding of multiplication another person might interpret as a lack of appreciation or understanding. This lack of objectivity is a serious impediment to a satisfactory teaching-learning situation. This is not to say that feelings and assumptions and interpretations do not exist. However, we must recognize that these nebulous, nonspecific terms must be made operational if they are to be dealt with successfully in the classroom.

TYPES OF BEHAVIOR

As we know from Psychology, there are two main types of human behavior. One type commonly known as respondent refers to a behavior which is actually caused by some stimulus. The other type of human behavior is called operant. This is a behavior that is not caused by a stimulus, but one which may be occasioned by the occurrence of a stimulus. For example, a puff of air in the eye actually **causes** the eye to blink. This is a respondent. However, a dog sitting on his master's command of "sit" is not a respondent because the master's saying "sit" does not actually cause a dog to sit. Sitting is an operant response because the verbal command of "sit" only **occasions** the dog's sitting. It can be said that the dog learns to sit because of the desirable consequences of sitting. To verify this point, you could easily demonstrate that a dog can be taught to sit on the verbal command of "stand up." Any verbal or physical stimulus can occasion a dog's sitting if the behavior results in something nice for the dog. Typically, the dog receives a reward for engaging in the desired behavior, and as the behavior becomes more firmly established, the rewards are systematically reduced. Those who are not familiar with the principles of behavior management tend to see the stimulus as causing the response, but in reality the behavior is strengthened by the consequences of the behavior.

Operant behaviors are not controlled by manipulating the stimulus, but rather by manipulating the consequences of the behavior. It can be simply understood by recognizing that when something pleasant follows a behavior, the behavior tends to increase. This simple principle of operant behavior can easily and successfully be applied to human behavior. For example, a young boy saying "please" is an operant response. In order to increase the frequency of his please-saying behavior, we need to increase the frequency of the desirable consequences which follow his saying "please." If the young boy says, "Please may I have a cookie?", and his saying "please" results in his obtaining a cookie, the frequency of please-saying behavior will increase. In the school situation, it remains the task of the teacher to identify desired behaviors and to identify and employ desirable consequences to that behavior.

If we think of everything we ask educationally handicapped children to do in school as a series of operant behaviors, it is possible to employ the principles of operant conditioning or behavior modification to facilitate a great deal of student learning. When we think of what we want our students to do, we are then able to easily formulate learning objectives for the students.

Successful teachers tend to state their objectives in terms of competencies that their students are expected to manifest. For example, a teacher's objective might be to increase the number of one digit numbers Trish successfully identifies in a five minute period. Suppose that Trish presently identifies two numbers correctly in a five minute period. If Trish subsequently identifies eight or more numbers correctly, she will have met the criterion as stated in the objective. This behavior should result in desirable consequences. A shrewd teacher will have previously determined what Trish views as desirable consequences. Suppose Trish really enjoys finger painting. The teacher can reinforce number identification behavior by allowing Trish to finger paint for ten or fifteen minutes subsequent to her meeting the criterion as stated in the objective.

EXAMPLES OF CONSEQUENCES

Desirable consequences can be anything a student likes, and these will serve to reinforce the behavior which immediately precedes it. Consequences is another name for reinforcers and there are a multitude of reinforcers available to the teacher. In order for a consequence to actually be a reinforcer, it must be truly desired by the student and delivered to the student immediately after the target behavior occurs.

The best way to find out if an activity is truly preferred by the student is to simply ask the student. As an alternative, ask each student to make up a list of preferred activities that he or she would like to have made available to him or her as the result of achieving target behaviors.

The problem of providing the reinforcement immediately can be a bit of a challenge to a busy teacher. A classroom strategy which makes this task less demanding and, in fact, very possible is the token economy or point system (Neef et al., 1992). In this system a point is recorded, a plastic chip is dropped in a cup or some other token is delivered to the student immediately upon his meeting the target behavior. These "tokens" can later be redeemed to treats, privileges, or activities.

Examples of reinforcers which can be used in class are:

Social
Gestures- a-ok
Good citizen award on desk
Facial expressions- smile
Word of approbation
Wink
Visit with nurse or librarian
Touch on the shoulder

Privileges
Access to free play area
Outside flag duty
Access to art area
Choosing the story to be read by teacher
Classroom monitor
Lead pledge of allegiance or song
Passing out supplies
Read directions for an activity to other children
Working on bulletin board
Listening to radio with ear plugs

Activities
Collecting papers
Tutoring another child
Watering plants
Helping in cafeteria or library
Feed animals
Operating slide projector
Erasing chalkboard
Running errands

In some cases, especially when an educationally handicapped child's repertoire of behavior is extremely low or very dependent, it is necessary to use reinforcers that are primary such as edible or con-

sumable reinforcers as opposed to secondary such as tokens or social praise. If primary reinforcers are needed to establish or maintain critical behaviors, then these are the types of reinforcers that should be employed. It is important for teachers to remember that they must not presume that a particular consequence is actually a reinforcer. The student's behavior will always reveal whether or not a particular consequence is indeed a reinforcer.

One term that may require elaboration is the term reinforcer. A reinforcer is simply a consequence, a thing which is added to the students' ecology. It could be positive, it could be aversive, but it is something that is added to the learner's ecology. If it is added immediately after a behavior occurs, it will affect that behavior (Strandy et al., 1979). Another term which must be distinguished from reinforcer is reinforcement. Reinforcement is the effect. In other words, it is what has happened as a result of that reinforcer being delivered (Winterling, 1990; Platt et al., 1980). Two terms that can be used to begin our consideration are the terms **positive reinforcement** and extinction. Positive reinforcement is when we add a pleasing consequence to the students' environment. The observed result is an increase in desired behavior. An example of positive reinforcement would be the teacher saying "good girl" for taking out her workbook. Any kind of positive reinforcement will increase behavior. A problem occurs when we make assumptions about what is a positive reinforcer. Just because something is a positive reinforcer to us does not mean that it will be to a child. Just because something is a positive reinforcer to Heather does not mean that it will be to Tamara. The test is: What is its effect on behavior? The other test is: Is it something a student likes or wants to do? If it is, it will serve as a positive reinforcer.

Parallel to positive reinforcement is the term extinction, which is an event that teachers need to understand fully. If we remove the pleasing consequence, in other words if we stop saying "good girl" after an appropriate behavior, the behavior will decrease and it will decrease dramatically–**unless** that behavior has been firmly established. Behavior must be solidly established or else it will be vulnerable to extinction.

The other side of the reinforcement model has to do with the use of aversive consequences. Just to make the model complete, adding an aversive consequence is known as **punishment**, and when punishment is used in the lab, human behavior decreases. Now in reality, punishment is not a viable option for most situations in which teachers are involved. First of all, punishment tends to suppress behavior more than to actually eliminate it, and secondly, teachers are not at liberty to use consequences that would legitimately be punishing. If they are just a little aversive, they are not going to work. If they are too aversive of course, we wouldn't ever want to use them.

That brings us to the term **negative reinforcement**, which is without question the most confusing term in behavior modification. It is *not* the same as punishment. It deals with the removal or the avoidance of an aversive consequence. When a student's behavior results in that student avoiding an aversive consequence, the behavior will increase, and this is known as negative reinforcement. A negative reinforcer is that which is applied in the condition of punishment or that which is removed or avoided in the condition of negative reinforcement. Keep in mind negative reinforcement is not punishment and under the condition of negative reinforcement behavior increases because the student has avoided an aversive consequence. If by finishing his social studies assignment Lamont has avoided staying in during recess or some other kind of aversive consequence, Lamont's social studies completion behavior will be strengthened. Avoiding such aversive consequences results in an increase or maintenance of behavior.

HOW TO DELIVER REINFORCEMENT

Teachers often are confused about how they should deliver consequences or reinforcers. In the behavioral literature, teachers sometimes can become very confused because it includes seemingly complicated topics like "schedules of reinforcement" (VanHouten & Nau, 1980). Very often it is reading about such things as schedules of reinforcement that convince us that they are far too complicated to use effectively in the classroom. This section will explain delivering reinforcers in a way that makes it understandable and will simplify it in a way that teachers can use effectively.

Basically, **fixed** or **established** or **consistent** schedules of reinforcement are used in establishing new behavior. For example, a continuous schedule of reinforcement–in other words, every time the behavior occurs a reinforcer is delivered–is the type of schedule that is used effectively for establishing new behaviors. The problem is, that if we reinforce every time, or so consistently that the student becomes used to it or expects it, it is very susceptible to extinction. If for some reason you were not able to deliver reinforcement on the same schedule, the behavior could extinguish or disappear very quickly.

Intermittent reinforcement is an explanation of the schedules of reinforcement that are used for maintaining a behavior. Once a behavior has become established, teachers want to maintain it by engaging in what is called *stretching the schedule.* If teachers are reinforcing every occurrence of a behavior, they might then move to reinforcing every other occurrence and then to every third or every fifth. Before long the students are on a completely intermittent schedule of reinforcement. Upon reflection, that is exactly what nature provides; that is what society provides. Most of the behaviors that students emit are in fact reinforced intermittently by their ecology, by their environment.

If teachers reinforce on a ratio schedule, what they're really doing is providing reinforcement contingent upon a certain number of behaviors. The number could be one, and they would be reinforcing on a continuous schedule. The number could be three, and they would reinforce every third occurrence. There are many behaviors that could be thought of that would be best served by using that type of reinforcement. The number of addition problems solved, the number of words spelled correctly, the number of art projects completed are but three examples. But there are other behaviors that are best reinforced on what is known as an interval schedule or by following a time schedule. Suppose that a teacher is interested in increasing the amount of time Hector stays on task. She might begin by providing a reinforcer every time Hector is working on task after one minute passes. Once that on-task behavior becomes established, she might increase the time to two minutes, five minutes, and then after a while she might have Hector on a completely intermittent schedule. Every now and then you reinforce him for two minutes of uninterrupted work, for eight minutes of uninterrupted work, or for five minutes of uninterrupted work.

DISCRIMINATIVE STIMULI

The type of stimulus that teachers need to be concerned with is called a **discriminative stimulus** which is a stimulus in whose presence a certain response is emitted. The response is not caused by the stimulus; the stimulus merely occasions the response (e.g., saying "sit" to a dog does not cause the dog to sit. Remember that you could just as easily teach the dog to sit when you say "stand up"). Since discriminative stimuli do not cause responses but merely occasion them, it can be seen how a teacher may become a discriminative stimulus for desired or undesired behavior. Discriminative stimuli are not automatic; rather they are learned by students. Consequently, Miss Jones may consider a class to be well behaved and very industrious students while Miss Smith may consider the same individuals to be rowdy. Just as teachers can become discriminative stimuli for student behavior, a section of the room may become a discriminative stimulus for playing and quiet activity or for group discussions or interactions (Marholin & Steinman, 1977).

When a particular teacher says to her students, "Take out your pencils and begin working," there is nothing about this command which actually causes them to comply. However, the students have learned that this particular behavior has consequences which may be considered desirable. They have also learned that alternative forms of behavior, such as refusing to begin work, talking and fooling around, or going to sleep may result in consequences which are extremely undesirable (e.g., missing recess, staying after school or being sent to the principal's office).

Looking at human behavior in this manner has many advantages, the major one being that it leads directly to a positive strategy of intervention. Because the determinants of human behavior are actual, observable factors of the environment, they are amenable to environmental manipulation which will result in the desirable behavior change. The best way to manage behavior is to manipulate aspects of the environment which are observable. It is impossible to work with hypothesized or imagined causes of behavior.

An example may help to make this situation more clear. The first task of teachers is to select a target. Suppose we decide to increase the frequency with which Nikki successfully spells her name. Next, we must identify the existing frequency with which she presently engages in the behavior. Lastly, we need to identify a desirable consequence; e.g., teacher attention. Now, if every time Nikki increases her existing frequency (even if only by one) the teacher dramatically praises and encourages her, the frequency of her name spelling behavior will increase. Needless to say, it is the teacher's responsibility to determine those consequences which the child views as desirable. Not all children will respond well to teacher praise. Some youngsters will work hard for chocolate candy while others are more likely to be motivated by free time.

THE APPLICATION OF CONSEQUENCES

It has hopefully been satisfactorily established that the consequences of a student's behavior determine the frequency of that behavior. It should be remembered that manipulating consequences is the same as delivering or not delivering reinforcement. By judiciously applying reinforcement, the teacher is providing the consequences for the student's behavior, and it soon becomes clear that it is possible for teachers to manage the behavior of their students for positive outcomes. The frequency of a behavior can be increased by positively reinforcing the behavior or by removing or preventing an aversive consequence which could follow the behavior. The frequency of a given behavior can be decreased by ignoring it (and insuring that others ignore it) or by positively reinforcing an incompatible behavior. For example, if a teacher wants to decrease the frequency of seat leaving he can positively reinforce sitting in a seat.

The manner in which consequences or reinforcers are delivered is technically known as schedules of reinforcement. However, schedules of reinforcement can appear to be an exceedingly technical topic to classroom teachers and appear to be entirely too complicated to include in the planning of their busy teaching day. Therefore, an attempt will be made to simplify the concept of schedules of reinforcement and make it easy for teachers to understand how to deliver or withhold reinforcement at the appropriate time.

Simply stated, schedules of reinforcement are either ratio, which means so much performance will result in a reinforcer, or interval, which means that so much time must pass before the reinforcer is delivered. The idea of course is to systematically remove the tangible reinforcers and help the students to manage their own behavior through an intrinsic reinforcement that they feel for a job well done. It should be emphasized that the appropriate goal for any user of behavior management techniques is **self-control** or **self-management** on the part of the student.

When a teacher is attempting to establish a brand new behavior in the student's repertoire (i.e. something the student has heretofore not done or performed) the best strategy is to reinforce every occurrence of that behavior. This is sometimes called a continuous schedule of reinforcement. After the behavior becomes firmly established, it would be advisable for the teacher to "stretch the schedule of reinforcement." In other words, start reinforcing every third occurrence of the behavior and then move to every fifth occurrence and ultimately move to what is called a variable schedule of reinforcement. With this schedule of reinforcement a teacher simply reinforces the behavior immediately after it occurs on a random schedule. Sometimes she'll reinforce the third occurrence and sometimes the sixth occurrence and then the next time it might be the fourth occurrence. Ultimately she will want to stretch the schedule so that you are only periodically providing tangible reinforcement to the behavior. When this stage is reached, a teacher can be assured that she has successfully established the behavior, and if she has truly stretched the schedule of reinforcement, she has done all in her power to make that behavior resistant to extinction (Platt et al., 1980).

An interval schedule of reinforcement is best when teachers are interested in including time in the target or behavioral objective. If a teacher wants to increase the amount of time a student stays on task or the amount of time which passes prior to some type of disruption, it would be appropriate to use an interval schedule of reinforcement. Once again, in establishing a new behavior it is best to reinforce consistently, such as every one minute or every two minutes. Once the teacher sees that the behavior is becoming established, it would be appropriate to move to what is known as a variable interval schedule. This simply means that he randomly reinforces the amount of time that the student is on task - continually increasing, however, the amount of time the student engages in the target behavior.

In summary, it can be said that a fixed schedule of reinforcement is best for establishing a behavior, and a variable schedule is best for maintaining a behavior. A choice between a ratio or performance based schedule of reinforcement and an interval or time based schedule is obviously determined by the circumstances of each situation.

USING BEHAVIOR MODIFICATION IN THE CLASSROOM

In order to be effective, behavior modification must be applied systematically and consistently. The first task of the teacher is to select the appropriate target . There must be two criteria present for a task to be an acceptable target. It must contain **observability** and **directionality**. If you can count the frequency of a behavior, the criterion of observability has been met. Directionality simply means that you intend to increase, decrease, or maintain the frequency of the behavior in question. For example, an appropriate target behavior might be to increase the frequency at which Melissa correctly spells her name. Once a target has been established, it is appropriate to formulate an objective or objectives relative to that target.

The next step is to determine the existing frequency of the child's particular behavior. In other words, how is the child currently performing on the task prior to any teaching intervention from the teacher? This procedure is commonly referred to as establishing the base rate or base line. Establishing the base rate is necessary because it provides the teacher a basis from which to evaluate the effectiveness of his or her teaching strategies. It is very important to be able to document that the strategies or other modifications of the learning ecology are being effective with the particular behavior. Teachers cannot allow this to be left to guess work or even to teacher judgment.

After a reasonable period of time for gathering a base rate, perhaps a week or ten days at the most, the teacher is ready to begin changing the consequences or providing consequences to the target behavior. These procedures were discussed earlier, but it should be emphasized that the consequences should be provided immediately upon the completion of the behavior.

With all tangible reinforcers, a teacher should also deliver social praise and encouragement. In time, it is the objective that the reinforcement will become intrinsic to the child, and he will continue to engage in appropriate behaviors for the satisfaction of a job well done or the intrinsic reinforcement of being successful. However, this does not happen overnight in educationally handicapped children, nor does it happen automatically. It is the teacher's responsibility to systematically remove the child from tangible reinforcers. This is referred to as stretching or extending the schedule of reinforcement. In other words, the teacher simply demands more work for increasingly lesser amounts of tangible reinforcement. In this way a youngster is not left exclusively dependent upon tangible reinforcement and in a position for a behavior to extinguish rather quickly.

The purpose of behavior modification is for the student to develop **self control** over all his or her own behaviors (Prater et al., 1992). This includes academic behaviors as well as social and deportment behaviors. Behavior modification is often necessary because many educationally handicapped children's academic behaviors exist at such a low frequency that the learner cannot function without some form of external reinforcement.

The final task of a teacher is to continue to keep accurate records of the student's performance. This is essential in order to determine whether the teaching strategies or modifications to the learning ecology which have been employed are successful. This aspect of keeping accurate records will be considered in greater detail in the next chapter.

REFERENCES

Bandura, A. (1977). *Social learning theory.* Englewood Cliffs, N.J.: Prentice Hall.

Burgess, R.L., Burgess, J.M., & Esveldt, K.C. (1970). An analysis of generalized imitation. *Journal of Applied Behavior Analysis, 3,* 39.

Espin, C.A., & Deno, S.L. (1989). The effects of modeling and prompting feedback strategies of sight word reading of students labeled learning disabled. *Education and Treatment of Children, 12,* 219-231.

Lalli, E.P., & Shapiro, E.S. (1990). The effects of self-monitoring and contingent reward on sight word acquisition. *Education and Treatment of Children, 13,* 129-141.

Luiselli, J.K., & Downing, J.N. (1980). Improving a student's academic performance using feedback and reinforcement procedures. *Education and Treatment of Children, 3,* 45-49.

Marholin, D. II, & Steinman, W.M. (1977). Stimulus control in the classroom as a function of the behavior reinforced. *Journal of Applied Behavior Analysis, 10,* 465-478.

Neef, N.A., Mace, F.C., Shea, M.C., & Shade, D. (1992). Effects of reinforcer rate and reinforcer quality on time allocation: Extensions of matching theory to educational settings. *Journal of Applied Behavior Analysis, 25,* 691-699.

Platt, J.S., Harris, J.W., & Clements, J.E. (1980). The effects of individually designed reinforcement schedules on attending and academic performance with behaviorally disordered adolescents. *Behavior Disorders, 5,* 197-205.

Prater, M.A., Hogan, S., & Miller, S.R. (1992). Using self-monitoring to improve on-task behavior and academic skills of an adolescent with mild handicaps across special and regular education settings. *Education and Treatment of Children, 15,* 43-55.

Strandy, C., McLaughlin, T.F., & Hunsaker, D. (1979). Free time as a reinforcer with high school special education students. *Education and Treatment of Children, 2,* 271-277.

Van Houten, R., & Nau, P.A. (1980). A comparison of the effects of fixed- and variable-ratio schedules of reinforcement on the behavior of deaf children. *Journal of Applied Behavior Analysis, 13,* 13-21.

Winterling, V. (1990). The effects of constant time delay, practice in writing in spelling, and reinforcement on sight word recognition in a small group. *Journal of Special Education, 24,* 101-116.

Chapter 6

PLANNING AND EVALUATING INSTRUCTION

DECIDING WHERE TO BEGIN

In deciding where to begin instruction with an educationally handicapped child, it is important for the teacher to initially determine the domain in which she will be working. Will she be working in the cognitive domain, the affective domain, or the psychomotor domain? The answer to this question is an important part of the planning process and helps the teacher begin to focus on the development of individualized learning objectives. It should be well-established in the minds of teachers and prospective teachers that good pedagogical planning requires careful teacher assessment of a curricular nature. Consequently the second important part of planning is a consideration of the data obtained from teacher assessment activities and how curriculum might subsequently be adapted (Simmons et al., 1991). An in-depth consideration of this topic was provided in Chapters 2 and 3.

Once this information has been obtained, it is appropriate to proceed with the formulation of specific instructional objectives for the tasks to be learned. It is a good idea to have prepared in advance possible subskills or prerequisites for each task. Having done this, the teacher should sequence them in the order that seems most logical. Deciding where a student fits into the instructional sequence is simply a matter of performing a task analysis on the material to be taught. In other words the task must be broken down into its component parts and sequenced from the easiest subtask to the most difficult subtask. Information regarding this process was covered in some detail in Chapter 4. Many teachers find it helpful to construct a simple checklist for the hierarchy of subskills which they have developed. A checklist gives the teacher an easy way to determine where in the hierarchy a particular educationally handicapped student might fit in terms of his individual strengths and weaknesses.

Not only does this procedure assist the teacher in developing individualized curriculum, it also aids the teacher in potentially grouping children for instruction. Children with similar deficiencies and curricular needs can often be grouped for those particular aspects of instruction. The last step in the process is to plan which instructional materials you will use to help a student meet his objectives. The selection of instructional materials is not an exact science and is often best determined by a good teacher's clinical judgment. The most important issue is that instructional materials should be selected because a teacher believes they are appropriate for a particular objective, not because they happen to be available in the classroom.

READINESS FOR INSTRUCTION

Readiness is a term that is often used in education but is frequently misunderstood by special educators, regular classroom teachers and administrators. Regrettably, it is also a term which is often used as a justification for not proceeding with instruction for a particular educationally handicapped child. Actually, any child is always ready to learn whatever comes next in the instructional hierarchy. If he has mastered the necessary prerequisite skills, he is ready for the next subtask in the hierarchy. Readiness must not be seen as a construct internal to the educationally handicapped child, which justifies not proceeding with appropriate instruction. It must not be seen exclusively as a developmental concept. Rather, readiness should be viewed as the mastery of the necessary prerequisite skills to a task. Teachers must never stop reminding themselves that they must develop programs to fit children and not expect children to fit into programs. If an educationally handicapped child isn't "ready" for a particular task, it means that prerequisite skills must become the target objectives.

INSTRUCTIONAL OBJECTIVES

Historically, it was generally recognized that the basic objectives of education were the development of:

1. citizenship
2. family life
3. moral and spiritual values
4. basic skills of communication
5. health and aesthetic expression
6. economic life.

More recently in Goals 2000: The Educate America Act, eight objectives were specified. These objectives are:

1. All children will begin school being prepared for learning.
2. America will have a high school graduation rate of 90 percent.
3. All Americans will be literate.
4. There will be an absence of drugs, guns, alcohol, and violence in our schools.
5. There will be a well educated teaching force.
6. Parents will be involved in their children's education.
7. America will be first in the world in science and mathematics achievement.
8. America will have high, world class academic standards for all students in the traditional academic disciplines.

As teaching objectives, these global statements sound lofty, but in fact are not particularly helpful. They are obviously too broad and too nebulous to be of any real value to teachers or students. They provide no indication of what to teach, how to teach it, or how to know when and if students have learned it. Equally important is the fact that these goals give no indication of what not to teach. They are so ambiguous and general that it is conceivable that almost any teaching activity could in some way be shown to be targeting one of these broad goals. Clearly such an outcome would be detrimental to the progress of educationally handicapped children.

If an instructional objective is to be of value, it must be attainable. In other words, a teacher must be able to determine if the objective or goal has in fact been met. An example of an attainable objective would be to teach all students in the class to orally recite the multiplication tables. It would be easy to determine if "yes" the students can recite the tables, or "no" they cannot recite them. To not have an appropriate level of specificity is to not have an objective which is truly attainable. For example, a statement such as "to develop the concept of multiplication" would not be attainable. It is not specific, and it does not give any indication of how and when the teacher will know that the students have met the objective. The secret is to avoid ambiguity and to strive for specificity.

Objectives should avoid terms such as "to know," "to understand," and "to appreciate"; and employ terms such as "to write," "to recite," and "to identify." Objectives should use verbs that are very specific and unquestionably observable.

Indeed the broad-based, general goals mentioned earlier sound as if they make for a well-rounded program, but all too often attempting to do a little of everything for everyone results in an inadequate job of teaching much of anything to anyone. The time available in a school day is precious, and this is especially true for the amount of time in a school day that can be devoted to instruction. Some studies have indicated that only one and one half hours per school day are devoted to instruction. It is not a question of not wanting to teach many things to all children; it is simply that we cannot. Therefore it is imperative that teachers limit themselves to the most important content skills and experiences which they determine are most beneficial to their educationally handicapped children.

The development of curriculum for a particular educationally handicapped child is a teacher decision. The decision does not rest with school districts or with school psychologists. Teachers must not blindly follow district curriculum guides for they are only general outlines and suggested sequences of content. However, they can be extremely helpful to a shrewd teacher in terms of helping her visualize the sequence of the skills and subskills in several particular content areas. The teacher herself must make a decision as to where the individual child fits in the instructional hierarchy based upon an evaluation of that child's individual pattern of strengths and weaknesses.

Curriculum is an individually determined set of objectives designed for each child. An instructional objective is a statement of expected student behavior which results from some teaching activity. This allows the teacher to know where she is going, when she gets there, and provides the child with information about what is expected of him. This striving for individuality and specificity eliminates assumptions and helps make the teacher accountable for her children's learning.

It has hopefully been sufficiently established that curriculum is not a general list of activities which can be used with all children. Rather, curriculum is an individually established set of objectives pertinent to each individual child based on that child's individual profile. The objectives that a teacher determines for an educationally handicapped child must reflect the most critical behavioral deficits in a child's repertoire of behavior. (i.e. academic behaviors, social behaviors, and affective behaviors).

CONSTRUCTING INSTRUCTIONAL OBJECTIVES

In order for a teacher to effectively interact with students and facilitate the learning process, it is necessary for her to specify instructional objectives for each student. An instructional objective is a statement of expected student behavior which results from some teaching activity. An instructional objective provides the teacher with information about where he is going with his lesson and more importantly lets him know when he has been successful. Most importantly, an instructional objective allows the students to know what is expected of them.

The conscientious and systematic use of objectives eliminates the necessity of making assumptions and inferences about student behavior. Similarly, student performance data on such objectives provides a meaningful indication of student progress and teacher accountability.

Components of Instructional Objectives

Instructional or behavioral objectives contain three basic elements. These elements are the *circumstance* or the situation in which you want the learner's *behavior* to occur, the behavior or specifically that which you want the learner to do, and the *criterion* or the degree of success that you will accept as an indication of the learner's success. Suppose you are interested in the number of two digit addition problems Kristin can solve. Your instructional objective might be:

When asked by the teacher (circumstance), Kristin will write the answers to two digit addition problems (behavior) with 90% accuracy (criterion).

This degree of specificity allows all concerned to know exactly what is expected. Further it provides the teacher with evidence for making decisions regarding curricular changes.

It should not be assumed that instructional objectives are appropriate only for strictly objective tasks. They should also be used for subjective assignments such as art, poetry writing, and group discussions. For example you might choose to develop an objective similar to the following for an art project:

After a field trip to a farm (circumstance), Cindy will draw a picture (behavior) to the teacher's satisfaction (criterion) of her most memorable experience.

Simply stated, objectives are specific statements of expected student behavior relative to the teacher-determined curriculum and instructional activities. Objectives are essential because it is the teacher's responsibility to determine what she is going to teach and what students are expected to learn prior to the start of each day. Unfortunately many teachers indicate by their own behavior that they feel that any and all teaching is inherently good. They imply that children will profit from whatever is presented in class. Careful consideration should be given to the conclusion that teaching is only valuable if it leads to student learning.

RECORD KEEPING

Evaluation of instruction is an important topic which teachers must address. Only the most irresponsible of teachers would not be concerned about whether a particular student was actually learning or whether or not particular instruction was being effective. These determinations can only be made by examining and considering student data. This of course means that student data needs to be collected, and that raises the issue of record keeping on the part of the teacher (Cohen et al., 1981).

It is imperative for teachers to understand from the very beginning that record keeping is not, and in fact must not be, an odious, time-consuming unpleasantry. To be of value to the teacher, record keeping must be both effective and efficient. In other words, it must be something the teacher can manage and it must result in information the teacher can readily use.

In the majority of cases teachers are interested in either the frequency of behavior or the duration of behavior. To be sure there are other measures, such as intensity, latency, or percent of interval, but most often teachers want to ascertain if a particular behavior is increasing, decreasing, or maintaining. For example, are the number of multiplication problems Heather successfully completes increasing? Are the number of disruptions Christy emits during art class decreasing? Is the amount of time Tamara stays on task during seat-work time maintaining or increasing?

In the majority of cases a teacher needs no more equipment to be a good record keeper than a pencil, a piece of paper and the clock on the wall. There is no question that the process can be enhanced by using a stop watch, a golf wrist counter or a tape recording of beeps or clicks at pre-set intervals. However, in order to be usable by teachers, it is best if the equipment is kept simple and the more complicated or sophisticated materials are avoided.

Teachers will find that most often the rate of behavior is the best indication of performance. Fortunately, the rate of student behavior is quite easy to calculate. Simply divide the number of behaviors observed by the number of minutes observed. If the target was time rather than frequency, the teacher or aide would similarly divide the time on task by the total time.

There is actually an easier way to observe and record behavior, and that is by using one (1) minute timed observations. Used regularly, over time, these one-minute timed observations have proven to be very reliable. Simply observe the student for one uninterrupted minute and record the number or amount of behavior observed. If these one minute observations occur daily, the teacher will have a reliable picture of the student's behavior in a matter of days.

If teachers are going to successfully determine whether or not a student's behavior has changed as a result of their intervention (teaching), it is imperative for them to know what the existing rate of behavior is prior to intervention.

The rate of behavior prior to any intervention on the part of the teacher is called the base line. Establishing a base line is necessary if we are going to make an informed judgment about whether our teaching is being effective. In other words, teachers need to know what the student is actually doing now, if they are to evaluate their teaching by looking at how well the student does after receiving and participating in the instructional activities.

Determining a Base Line

Let's assume we are interested in the number of long division problems Lisa correctly solves. Before we attempt to improve the rate of her long division performance, we need to know the current rate at which Lisa solves long division problems. The current rate of performance is the base rate or base line.

All you would need to do is to give Lisa an opportunity to solve long division problems for about five days. On each of these days, the teacher would take a one minute timed sample and record the data on a properly identified chart (see Figure 6.1).

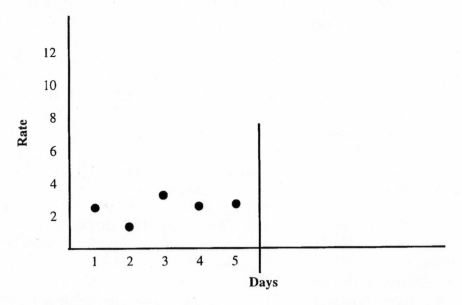

Figure. 6.1 Rate at which Lisa correctly solves long division problems.

Now the teacher has a clear indication of Lisa's current level of performance and is in an ideal position to evaluate the effectiveness of his intervention strategies.

Intervention

At this stage the teacher makes an environmental manipulation such as changing the schedule of reinforcement, switching instructional materials or modifying the instructional objective and continues to record daily one minute timed observations. If the rate of long division problem solving increases, the environmental manipulation was effective, and if the rate does not increase, further environmental manipulations on the part of the teacher will be required.

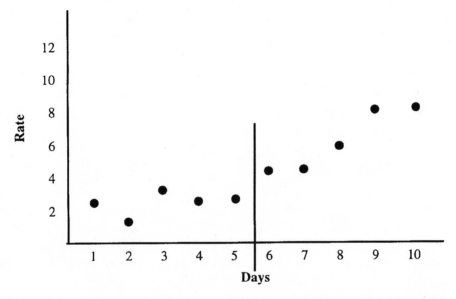

Figure 6.2. Rate at which Lisa correctly solves long division problems after intervention.

Once the behavior stabilizes the teacher needs to decide if further environmental manipulation is required or if it is time for her to move on to another objective (such as long division problems with a remainder).

Another example would be the amount of time Darwin remains on-task during seat work. Remember the teacher can use one minute timed observations or the percentages of any observation time to ascertain the rates.

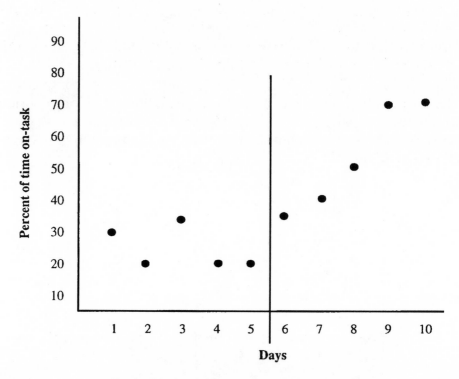

Figure 6.3. Rate of Darwin's on-task behavior.

It is important to remember that record keeping is not an activity which consumes an inordinate amount of teacher time. It is nonetheless a very important activity and one which teachers must develop skill and facility in performing. Teachers must put themselves in the position of knowing whether or not what they are doing is being effective. Frequently the process can be facilitated by having the students engage in self-recording (Blick & Test, 1987; Lloyd et al., 1989; Lloyd et al., 1982; Paquin, 1978).

REFERENCES

Blick, D.W., & Test, D.W. (1987). Effects of self-recording on high school students' on-task behavior. *Learning Disability Quarterly, 10*, 203-213.

Cohen, R., Polsgrove, L., Rieth, H., & Heinen, J.R.K. (1981). The effects of self-monitoring, public graphing, and token reinforcement on the social behaviors of underachieving children. *Education and Treatment of Children, 4*, 125-138.

Lloyd, J.W., Bateman, D.F., Landrum, T.J., & Hallahan, D.P. (1989). Self-recording of attention versus productivity. *Journal of Applied Behavior Analysis, 22,* 315.

Lloyd, J.W., Hallahan, D.P., Kosiewicz, M.M., & Kneedler, R.D. (1982). Reactive effects of a self-assessment and self-recording on attention to task and academic productivity. *Learning Disability Quarterly, 5,* 216-227.

Paquin, M. (1978). The effects of pupil self-graphing on academic performance. *Education and Treatment of Children, 15,* 43-55.

Simmons, D.C., Fuchs, D., & Fuchs, L.S. (1991). Instructional and curricular requisites of mainstreamed students with learning disabilities. *Journal of Learning Disabilities, 24* (6), 354-359.

Chapter 7

LITERACY

Before becoming specifically involved in individual academic content areas, it seems appropriate to quickly review basic teaching strategies that are appropriate in all content areas with educationally handicapped children. By now it should be clear to the reader that the route to success with educationally handicapped children is individualizing their instruction. Their instruction is individualized by the teacher engaging in teacher assessment activities and by the teacher assessing the student's entire learning ecology. This process is often referred to as *clinical teaching*. The individual patterns of strengths and weaknesses for each educationally handicapped student are identified; and subsequently, specific learning objectives are stated by the teacher for each student. It is imperative to remember that two children who are underachieving at exactly the same level may in fact, be underachieving for very different reasons. Therefore, it is inappropriate to assume that the same instructional strategies and objectives will work for both children. It must be remembered that in order for a teacher to engage in teacher assessment activities it is necessary for that teacher to fully understand and be comfortable with the process of task analysis. In order for a teacher to be successful at analyzing the tasks which make up a particular objective, it is necessary for that teacher to have some sense of the appropriate sequence of instruction. It is far less important to have identified the exact sequence than it is to have identified a logical sequence which makes sense to the teacher. This sequence gives the teacher a road map to follow in building task upon task to reach a specific objective.

Once the instructional objectives have been identified it is appropriate to employ strategies such as direct instruction where the lessons are taught by the teacher directly to the learner. After specific objectives have been mastered it is sometimes appropriate to use less direct activities such as peer tutoring, computer assisted instruction and cooperative learning. These activities are best when used by teachers of educationally handicapped students for practicing the skills and tasks which students have recently mastered.

Sometimes it is necessary to create and establish motivation in students who heretofore have shown little interest in academic pursuits. This can be done effectively by employing the strategies outlined in Chapter 5. Teachers often must attempt to establish specific intrinsic/extrinsic motivation in their educationally handicapped students. Once the teacher is successful in establishing motivation for specific tasks by using extrinsic reinforcers, it is possible and in fact quite probable that more generalized, intrinsic, motivation will occur.

In terms of specific suggestions, teachers are encouraged, where possible, to work one-on-one or in small groups with the individual educationally handicapped child, to directly teach the child the individual tasks in the learning hierarchy, to provide students with sufficient time to reach mastery, to allow the children to practice frequently and to liberally reinforce successful performance.

READING

Reading is unquestionably one of the most important curricular considerations teachers of the educationally handicapped must address. Frost and Emery (1996) indicate that from 5 percent to 6 percent of all school age children have developmental reading disabilities. Reading and language are interrelated, and disability in one is related to disability in the other. Opportunities for practicing oral language are continuous in the environments of most children. It is natural and seen as valuable by the child. On the other hand, "Fluent reading requires the reader to automatically apply his linguistic competence, as well as a plethora of word-attack skills, reading habits, and experiences to the visual material in order to obtain meaning" (Orlando, 1973, p. 263).

Remediation of reading disabilities is enhanced by individualized instruction (Orr, 1989; McCormick, 1994) and direct instruction (Stephans, 1993; Allen, 1990). Haynes and Jenkins (1986) suggest that a reader's self-esteem improves when provided with individualized instruction, and Rieth, et al. (1977) have established that reading achievement can be improved with the use of contingent free time. Remediation in reading involves hard work on the part of the teacher and student, sufficient time dedicated to the process, and active participation on the part of the learner. "Student learning is related to time on task, but there is a distinction between the time allocated for learning by the teacher and the time in which the student actually participates in learning. The engagement of the student in the learning task thus becomes a major goal of instruction, and in direct teaching, the classroom learning environment is structured to bring this about" (Lewis, 1983, p. 234).

There are an endless number of programs and methodologies devoted to the remediation of reading disabilities. Frost and Emery (1986) offer some general intervention strategies which include:

- teach meta-cognitive strategies
- provide direct instruction in language analysis and the alphabetic code
- discuss the specific purposes and goals of each reading lesson
- provide regular practice with reading materials that are contextually meaningful
- teach for comprehension
- teach reading and spelling in conjunction
- provide positive, explicit, and corrective feedback

These intervention strategies are intended to serve as *general* guidelines for remediation. It will nevertheless be necessary to employ *specific* instructional strategies to meet the individual objectives established for each learner. It is well-known that the strategies for teaching reading are legion, and care must be exercised when selecting or designing a program of reading instruction. It is easy to let the textbook and instructional materials representatives make such decisions, but that strategy is clearly not in the best interest of the learner. "Teaching students to read is not an easy task; nor is there one best method for teaching reading. Teachers need to know a variety of techniques and have access to different materials for teaching" (Mandelbaum, 1989, p. 89).

In selecting an approach, the teacher should remember that her effectiveness is more important than the particular method chosen. Therefore, the teacher should select a program with which she is comfortable. Also important is the teacher's belief about how reading skills are learned. For example, if a teacher believes that reading develops through phonetic analysis and word-attack skills, she would not want to employ a program that emphasizes sight words or exclusively linguistics.

LANGUAGE

Reading is an important aspect of literacy, but the total concept of literacy also includes a consideration of how language develops in a child. The components of language are typically thought to include:

PHONOLOGY: The study of sounds and the rules for combining sounds to form words (e.g., vowels, consonants, blends).

MORPHOLOGY: The study of word formation involving the combination of sounds to form words.

SYNTAX: The rules for combining words into sentences.

SEMANTICS: The meaning attached to symbols (i.e., written language).

PRAGMATICS: The social use of language (using language in various contexts).

METHODS FOR IMPROVING PHONOLOGICAL SKILLS

The development of phonological skills is critical to educationally handicapped children (Yoshimoto, 1997; Beginning Reading and Phonological Awareness, 1996). In order for an educationally handicapped student to be able to read, a strong foundation in phonological skills must be developed. Phonological ability can be seen as the ability to identify and manipulate the sounds of language (Adams, Kameenui, Lyon, Smith, & Stanovich, 1996). The National Center for the Tools of Education has designed principles that develop to support phonological awareness and beginning reading which include what are known as **conspicuous strategies** (Chard, Kameenui, & Simmons, 1994).

In order to identify and understand words, a child must be able to hear and manipulate sounds in language. **Conspicuous strategies** are used to promote this phonological awareness, and they are the steps in beginning reading that lead to effective word recognition. Specifically they are the steps a reader takes to recognize and remember the sound structures of a word (Chard et al., 1994). Conspicuous strategies such as *segmenting, blending, rhyming, and emphasizing morphemes* help the educationally handicapped learner in the complicated process of beginning reading.

Segmentation involves the relationship of a whole to its parts. For example, teachers explain how sentences can be segmented into individual words. The students begin with a complete sentence and, through segmenting, are taught that the sentence consists of individual words. Similarly, educationally handicapped children are shown that multi-syllable words can be segmented into syllables. Once educationally handicapped students have achieved some degree of success on segmenting, phonemes can be introduced. Specific sounds can be modeled by the teacher and students are asked to produce the sound in isolation and subsequently in words (Adams et al., 1996).

Blending is a skill that virtually all students are taught, but one that is difficult for educationally handicapped students to master. Blending is the process of making individual sounds in a word and blending them together. For example, the word DOG is given to a student who must identify each individual sound and blend them together to pronounce the word.

Rhyming is an important phonemic strategy with which educationally handicapped students also have difficulty. Oldrieve (1997) has developed a structured spelling method that helps students develop the ability to rhyme with the intention that it will help them become better decoders, readers, and spellers. Two smaller conspicuous strategies are subsumed in this spelling strategy, *compare and contrast* and *words-on-the-wall. Compare/contrast* requires that students locate an unknown word in their text. They then have to find a word with a similar ending from their word bank and use this word to help decode the unknown word. Words-on-the-wall consist of rhyming vocabulary flashcards hung on the wall. Students orally read the words and refer to them when needed.

Another conspicuous strategy is the teaching of *morphomes*, which are the smallest meaningful units of language. Understanding morphomes helps to develop mastery in decoding and encoding the multitude of sounds and syllables which appear in beginning reading.

As phonological awareness develops, it is reinforced through instruction in the use of prefixes, suffixes, and Latin/Greek roots.

According to Yoshimoto (1997), about 50 percent of the English language comes from Latin roots, and instruction of Latin roots provides educationally handicapped children the opportunity to understand hundreds of words through derivatives.

STRATEGIES FOR BEGINNING READING

Once an educationally handicapped child has achieved some degree of success in phonological awareness, he/she is ready to begin the actual process of reading.

Instruction for Younger Children

An approach to remedial reading which has proven successful over time, especially in the first two years of reading instruction, is the phonics approach. In this approach, the teacher would teach the educationally handicapped student the most common sound for a group of letters and letter combinations. These letter-sound correspondences are practiced in the context of vocabulary words and in sentences as soon and as often as possible. Grossen and Carnine (1993) offer the following steps for phonics instruction for educationally handicapped children:

1. Introduce letter-sound correspondence in isolation.
2. Teach students to blend sounds, to read words. Model the way sounds blend together into words. Sound out words and then match to actual words from the students' vocabulary. Begin practice blending sounds as soon as the student is secure in at least two separate sounds.
3. Provide immediate feedback on oral reading errors. Concentrate on oral reading rather than silent reading because in silent reading, it is extremely difficult, if not impossible, to correct errors. Listen to the child read orally and give corrective feedback during the reading exercise.
4. Provide extensive practice. Have the student practice new sounds in isolation every day for several days and then incorporate the sounds into word-reading activities.

Another strategy that has proven to be successful with beginning reading is called **assisted reading**. With this strategy, a student listens to a taped passage while following the written word with his/her finger. Subsequently the student reads along with the teacher, and finally reads the passage independently. Gilbert, McLaughlin, and Williams (1996) observe that studies in the area of assisted reading document an increase in the number of words read correctly and a decrease in the number of words read incorrectly. Assisted reading improves reading fluency, which enables the learner to progress from the point of beginning reading to being able to read a story and actually obtain meaning from it.

Approaches for Older Students

For older students, Saski and Carter (1984) suggest assessment procedures which include:

1. Modified miscue analysis in which the teacher identifies the error patterns in oral reading
2. The use of informal reading inventory consisting of a series of graded passages read aloud in sequence until the student begins to make a given number of reading errors. Subsequently, comprehension questions are asked orally at the end of each passage.
3. The cloze procedure, in which the teacher would delete a particular word from content area passages. This provides emphasis on discerning intended meaning of what is read.

They also offer the following instructional suggestions:

1. The use of advance organizers. This helps relate new material to previously learned material prior to a selection being read.
2. Previewing, which is effective in introducing students to reading materials and helping them find the reason for reading the passage. This process would include:
    a. Selecting key words and major concepts for preview
    b. Presenting the major elements in a systematic related manner
    c. Apply previewed material to reading the passage during instruction
3. Guided reading. This would include:
    a. Preparing student for reading assignment
    b. Silent reading and oral retelling
    c. Return to the material for more information
    d. Organize remembered information
    e. Provide questions to establish relationships
    f. Test students on information read.

4. Directed reading-thinking activities which is an activity designed primarily for small group instruction. It includes the following steps:
   a. Predicting–to enable students to define the reasons for reading a passage
   b. Reading to select relevant information for purposes previously determined by the teacher
   c. Evaluating and revising predictions made based on information read
5. Study strategies:
   a. SQ3R–Survey, Question, Read, Recite, Review
   b. Focus on the organization and features of the books and materials being read

STRATEGIES FOR PROMOTING AND INCREASING READING COMPREHENSION

One of the most important and yet difficult areas to remediate is the area of comprehension. One can conclude from Swason (1981) that comprehension performance is difficult to improve and improvement is enhanced by identifying comprehension as an instructional objective and a dependent variable. "Many learning disabled children reach the regular classroom without the comprehension proficiency necessary to deal with the tasks demanded by the school curriculum" (Swanson, 1981, p. 189). In order for an educationally handicapped child to acquire proficiency in reading comprehension, many strategies can be utilized. **Modeling** and **guided practice** are standard methodological strategies for building reading comprehension.

All types of reading comprehension strategies are enhanced when they are **modeled** explicitly by the teacher. Billingsley and Ferro-Almeida (1993) point out, "Modeling is critical to the teaching-learning process because it is the means by which students gain insight into how reading skills are to be performed" (p. 276). Once a teacher has modeled a strategy, students need to be provided an opportunity to practice this skill under the supervision and guidance of the teacher. This **guided practice** should be a period of frequent positive and corrective feedback from the teacher to the students.

In order for a student to comprehend, she needs to be able to relate the new information to her own existing repertoire of knowledge. Comprehension can be viewed as an interaction between newly acquired information and a student's existing body of knowledge. If a student can make connections with new material and make it familiar, the likelihood of comprehension is increased. If educationally handicapped students do not have adequate **prior knowledge** about a particular subject, the teacher is called upon to provide sufficient background so that the learner can make the necessary connections.

REMEDIAL READING PROGRAMS

There have been federally funded programs established whose purpose is, at least in part, the remediation of reading deficits. "In response to school failure generally, and reading failure specifically, two separate federally initiated instructional support programs have emerged. Instructional support programs for the disadvantaged under Chapter 1, and resource room programs for the mainstreamed mildly handicapped under EHA are designed to address achievement deficits through specialized instructional services" (Allington & McGill-Franzen, 1989, p. 539).

"The most striking difference is in the instruction in the regular education program. The mainstreamed mildly handicapped students received 35 minutes a day less reading/language arts instruction than the Chapter 1 students in their regular education classrooms. Although special education students received more minutes of special reading instruction than Chapter 1 students, the amount was not large enough to offset the differences between the groups in the regular education program. Thus, mainstreamed special education students received fewer minutes of reading instruction across the school day than did Chapter 1 students" (Allington & McGill, 1989, p. 538).

Clearly the issue of how remedial reading instruction is delivered to educationally handicapped students is an issue of primary importance. The educationally handicapped student is best served when provided with instruction supplemental to the basic program. For the lowest-achieving readers, cross-age peer tutoring and supplemental instruction were necessary for improvement (Jenkins et al., 1994). In such situations, a natural concern arises about the impact on the other students in the class. This concern, while understandable, is unfounded. "Apparently, our efforts to create instructional accommodations (peer tutoring, cooperative learning, heterogeneous groups) for struggling students did not detract from the achievement from more able students" (Jenkins et al., 1994, p. 356).

The educationally handicapped student is best served when reading is supplemented in a resource room and does not supplant reading in the regular classroom (Haynes and Jenkins, 1986). Supplemented instruction for students with reading difficulties is more the rule than the exception. "We take some comfort in knowing that other researchers who have achieved success in accommodating individual differences have had to add some form of intense supplemental assistance over and above the classroom reading programs" (Jenkins et al., 1994, p. 355).

According to Haynes and Jenkins (1986) many regular and special education teachers who share students believe that the resource room program of reading instruction is the primary means by which special education will learn to read. Haynes and Jenkins (1986) indicate that increasing the amount of time devoted to reading instruction will assist educationally handicapped children in reading achievement, and they specifically suggest that reading instruction should be provided both in the regular classroom and in the resource room setting. The resource room teacher and the classroom teacher must collaboratively establish a "game plan" for each student they share. They must both be working on the same objectives, employing a consistent methodology, and providing feedback to each other regarding the students' progress.

Consistency is important not only in methodology but also in the overall approach to addressing the students' academic deficits. Individualized instruction jointly developed and jointly delivered by the special education and regular classroom teacher is precisely what is needed by the educationally handicapped child. Ekwall (1986) has identified some important remedial procedures appropriate for individualized instruction in the area of reading:

1. Make sure the reading program is highly individualized. It should be directed toward correcting certain reading deficiencies that would be manifested in a task analysis. In other words, find out what the child is weak in and work on that area, as opposed to a broad-based general approach to reading.
2. Start with the student's strongest area. This will help build the child's confidence. Once confidence and rapport are established, the teacher can begin incorporating material and skills which are not known by the child.
3. Help the reader to recognize and verbalize the problem. This will allow the student to see what is wrong, what the problem is, and what needs improvement. For example, tape record a child reading and have the child listen to and identify the deficiencies he hears.

4. Make the reader aware of progress. For example, show the reader the difference in the number of errors made today from the number of errors made yesterday. Perhaps create a "Gee Whiz" chart (a chart which dramatically emphasizes even the slightest improvement in graph form).

5. Make the learning process meaningful to the student. Try to explain to the student and help him understand why learning sight words is important or why development of comprehension skills are important.

6. Use appropriate materials which are individual to the learner. Pick materials to match the objectives that you have set for each child.

7. Continue assessment as you teach. Continually employ the process of diagnostic teaching. The more you teach, the more information you will uncover about what the child needs in terms of subsequent remediation.

8. Maintain a relaxed attitude. Try to refrain from appearing too authoritative. The more relaxed and comfortable the learner is, the more likely he will achieve success.

9. Provide evidence of your confidence in the student's ability. Help the student feel confident in his ability to be successful.

10. Help the student develop skill in the process of self-instruction so that learning can continue on a more independent and self-directed manner.

11. Provide follow-up. Each time you conclude a lesson, review what you learned and reinforce the major objectives with the learner.

READING RECOVERY PROGRAM

A unique and very effective program designed to remediate reading difficulties is known as Reading Recovery. "Reading Recovery is different from traditional remedial programs. It begins early, provides intensive one-to-one help, provides long-term special training for teachers, focuses on strengths instead of deficits, immerses the child in reading and writing rather than drilling on skills and 'items' of knowledge, expects accelerated progress from the lowest achievers, and requires that the instructional program be adjusted to each child's strengths" (Pinnell, 1989, p. 161).

As suggested earlier in the chapter, regular classroom instruction in reading is not a sufficient amount of instructional time and not a sufficient degree of curricular emphasis for many educationally handicapped children. "Experience in regular classrooms alone is not sufficient for some children. For one thing, much research indicates that many low-SES students are at a disadvantage in the mass education taking place in schools and classrooms" (Pinnell, 1989, p. 162). It isn't that such instruction is poor or inappropriate; it is simply that some children need more time on task to adequately develop necessary literacy skills. Reading Recovery is a program that addresses these important issues of time and emphasis. "It is particularly important for at-risk children to have many opportunities to explore and relate the two processes; thus, reading and writing are used together in the program" (Pinnell, 1989, p. 169).

Reading deficiency is an academic problem of extraordinary importance because "children who do not learn to read by the end of first grade will fail to achieve in almost all other areas of the school curriculum" (Boehnlein, 1987, p. 32). Not only will children have academic problems, but students who leave school unable to read will become a social liability because they will be lacking the basic skill needed to support themselves in making an economic contribution to society (Boehnlein, 1987).

Learning literacy skills is an active, purposeful activity and many educationally handicapped children do not have the literacy experiences in their learning ecologies to provide a foundation for the literacy instruction they will receive in school. They are not read to, encouraged to develop expressive language, or encouraged to listen with discrimination and to think about what they've heard. Even in the most ideal of situations, some children experience difficulty in effectively learning to read and use language.

Reading Recovery Strategies

To the degree possible, emphasis should be given to preventing literacy problems or to addressing them as early in a child's school life as possible. The sooner an educationally handicapped child catches up, the more effective and efficient will be his learning in all academic subjects.

Nothing can take the place of good teaching in the regular classroom. However, even the best teachers have students who are not making enough progress in reading and require special help.

Reading Recovery is a structured program designed to accelerate the progress of young children who are at risk of failure in learning to read. Students are chosen from the bottom twenty percent of their first grade classes. An individual diagnostic survey is used to check for let-

ter identification, sight words, concepts about print, writing vocabulary, phoneme awareness, and running record of text reading to
choose students for this program. The program is based on two
assumptions. The first assumption is that detailed observations of how
a child reads and writes should be the basis for identifying what the
child already knows and also what the child needs to learn. The second assumption is that the reading behaviors exhibited by good readers can be taught to those students who do not pick them up on their
own.

Reading Recovery is designed to accelerate student progress and to
bring them "up to speed" with the rest of the class, and it is based on
the view of children as active learners. It is not designed as a classroom
program, but is something extra intended to be used with good classroom teaching.

In addition to classroom instruction, Reading Recovery students are
taught in a one-to-one situation for 30 minutes daily by a teacher who
has been specifically trained in Reading Recovery techniques. Each
lesson includes five basic components. The first is reading known stories. Students may read four or five little books with which they have
previously been successful. These books are based on natural language patterns. The second component is trading a story that was read
on time the previous day. While the student is reading this story, the
Reading Recovery teacher is analyzing the student's reading using a
running record. The next part of the session involves writing a sentence or story. The teacher guides the student in writing his/her own
sentence/story. Through this exercise students are learning to hear
sounds in words and gradually spell them correctly. The fourth component includes working with a cut-up sentence from the story. The
child is asked to put the sentence in correct order and read it to the
teacher. The final step is introducing and reading a new book that will
be reread tomorrow for the running record assessment (Pinnell, 1989,
1990).

During the entire lesson there is a strong emphasis on the relationship between the reading and writing process. Students are taught to
use effective strategies that strong readers use, such as using picture
and context clues, cross-checking meaning, self-monitoring, self-cor-
recting, using beginning sounds, using known words and language patterns, as well as repetition. The major goal of Reading Recovery is to
teach students strategies that will help them become independent

readers and which they will be able to use to learn at a regular level in their classroom and throughout their life. In order to do this, Reading Recovery teachers always start with what the child knows, and build on that to learn the unknown. In fact, the first few sessions of Reading Recovery are known as "Roaming the Known." During this time, the teacher spends most of the time just getting to know the student and what he/she knows already. This helps the teacher analyze what skills he/she can build upon. Reading Recovery teachers lead students through their readings by reminding them of strategies and constantly asking students which strategies they used to figure out a particular word. In addition to constantly asking students to explain what they did, teachers constantly praise students for strategies they use correctly during reading. Teachers often model the thinking for the child, but rarely read the word for him/her (Pinnell, 1989, 1990 ; Ross et al., 1995; Hiebert, 1994).

Several key factors of Reading Recovery have been proven to be effective. Reading Recovery is based on the theory that reading emphasizes meaning. The program involves reading connected or "real text." Reading Recovery provides children with more time to learn necessary reading strategies. These students receive more instruction in reading than their classmates, which gives them the opportunity to accelerate more quickly so that they can catch up and make average progress in the classroom.

Pinnell (1989) conducted research to determine whether Reading Recovery had been effectively implemented. He chose the lowest students in the first grade classes. After completion of the program, he found Reading Recovery students when compared to a comparable control group to score higher on concepts of print, writing vocabulary, a dictated sentence checking for phonetic skills, and text level reading. A goal of Reading Recovery is that students will continue to make progress and use the skills learned. Pinnell also did a follow-up study with these same children. At the end of the second year, Reading Recovery students still scored higher that the comparison group on the dictated sentence and text reading.

INFORMAL ASSESSMENT OF READING AND LISTENING COMPREHENSION

Scenario: A first-grade class and Mrs. Jones is interested in the students' abilities in the area of literal reading comprehension (who, what, and when-type questions only).

Behavioral Objective: After reading the paragraph silently, the student will write the answers to the questions about the paragraph with 80 percent or better accuracy.

Reading is one of the fundamental skills that students are expected to acquire, and students who are having difficulty with reading are almost always having trouble in other academic areas as well. Consequently, reading comprehension can be seen as one of the basic building blocks to successful learning in all academic areas.

To assess literal reading comprehension, Mrs. Jones will begin with a classroom warm-up activity which will assess literal listening comprehension. It has several purposes:

1. It focuses the students' attention.

2. It provides a baseline of comparison on listening comprehension/reading comprehension.

3. It presents a clear picture of what I am asking them to do.

First the students and Mrs. Jones will go through a paragraph together as a class. Mrs. Jones will read the following paragraph to the students:

Todd made this valentine today.

It is red and pretty.

It has lace on it.

His grandfather will like it.

Then she will show an overhead with the written words that were just read to the class, and a cartoon illustrating the written words.

Next, Mrs. Jones will orally ask the question about the literal content of the paragraph, and will ask each student to write down his/her response on a piece of paper. After providing reasonable time to write down their responses, she will randomly call on different students to read aloud their written response. As each question is answered, Mrs. Jones will uncover the written question on the overhead and will write in the answer the student gives to the question. If a student gives an incorrect answer, she will prompt that student to come up with the correct answer by asking them to review the paragraph. If the student cannot correctly answer the question, Mrs. Jones will call on another student to assist.

Throughout this entire process Mrs. Jones will be observing the students and making any necessary assessment notes. The students will not see the written question until they have already responded. They will have only heard the following questions about the paragraph:
1. What is on the valentine?
2. What is red?
3. Who made the valentine?
4. When did Todd make it?
5. Who will get the valentine?

After going through this warm-up as a class, Mrs. Jones will collect each student's paper with his/her answers to the warm-up questions and will hand out seat work with another paragraph and set of questions. This time she will not read the paragraph aloud. The students will be given ample time to read the paragraph silently and answer the questions about the paragraph.

Initially Mrs. Jones will collect each student's paper with his/her work. If a student has incorrectly answered a question or questions, she will make a note of which question it is (is it a who, what, or when question?). Mrs. Jones will look for any pattern to the incorrect answers. If the student had difficulty answering most of the questions, she will look at his/her answers to the oral warm-up and see if the problem exists there as well. If it does not, she has a reasonable clue that the problem lies within the actual *reading* of the paragraph, and perhaps not so much in the comprehension. Of course it would be appropriate to gather several more pieces of data before coming to any conclusion.

If all of the students meet the behavioral objective (80 percent mastery), Mrs. Jones would probably retest them again within the next few days before going on to the next objective.

Outcome A:
Johnny had difficulty with both the oral warm-up and the written seat work.

Mrs. Jones would want to take a step back with Johnny, and assess his listening comprehension at a more basic level. She would also want to investigate whether Johnny was having a problem with attention. She would read him a short sentence such as the following:

The cat woke up from his nap and walked out the door.

Then she could show Johnny two pictures: One illustrating the cat waking up and one illustrating the cat walking out the door. She would ask Johnny to point to the picture that happened first and then to the picture that happened next.

Outcome B:

Sally had no difficulty with the warm-up, but she missed most of the seat work questions.

Mrs. Jones could ask Sally to read the paragraph on the handout. Can she read the paragraph with ease or is she having much difficulty? What is her rate of reading? Is she concentrating so hard on the identification of the words that she is unable to focus on the content?

WORKSHEET

Name_____Date_____

Mary got a new hat today.
It has a flower on it.
Her mother gave it to her.
It is blue and white.

1. What is on the hat?

_____

2. Who got the hat?

_____

3. When did Mary get the hat?

_____

4. Who gave Mary her new hat?

_____

5. What color is Mary's hat?

_____

INFORMAL ASSESSMENT OF ORAL READING PROBLEMS

Scenario: Mrs. Smith's second grade class has four reading groups of different reading abilities. At the beginning of the year Mrs. Smith decided that she was going to screen her reading groups for specific problems that occur in beginning readers.

Objective: The purpose of this activity is to identify possible reading problems at an early stage.

Method:

1. Mrs. Smith felt it was important to initially define what she was looking for. She found that the following areas were the most significant and frequently occurring oral reading problems:

    a. Omission

    b. Substitution

    c. Pronunciation

    d. Repetition

    e. Insertion

2. She then made up a checklist of these problem areas that could be used while she was teaching her reading lesson to a specific reading group.

3. Mrs. Smith then selected a book that she felt would be fun for the children to read, and one that would also be on the childrens' reading level.

4. After working out these plans for her Assessment, she was ready to assess the students.

Procedure:

Step 1

1. Have each student in the reading group read the same paragraph aloud.

2. Tally on the checklist how many times the student made a mistake. If the same word is being missed, write down that word.

Step 2

1. Meet individually with the students who had difficulties in one or more of these areas.

2. Have the child pick a favorite story from a list of books that you had already chosen.

3. Ask the child to read a part of that story. While the child is doing this, mark the mistakes in the specific areas on your checklist.

4. After the child has read the passage, the teacher can read the rest of the story to the child.

At the conclusion of these steps, Mrs. Smith will have a reasonable idea of where the child needs help in reading. It is important to note that the second part of the assessment needs to be completed, because the child who did poorly on the first day may just have had a bad day. When the teacher knows what the problem area is, she could help the child individually or assign group work or cooperative learning activities that will address the child's individual needs.

The purpose of this assessment activity is to define problem areas a student may have in reading. The information that will be gained from this activity will help a teacher plan activities to remediate and hopefully solve the problem before the student moves to a subsequent objective.

REFERENCES

Allen, D. (1991). A literacy program improvement plan for low achieving first-graders using reading recovery strategies. ERIC Document Reproduction Service ED 329945.

Allington & McGill-Franzen. (1989). School response to reading failure: Instruction for Chapter 1 and special education students in grades two, four, and eight. *The Elementary School Journal, 89*, 529-542.

Beginning reading and phonological awareness for students with learning disabilities. (1996). Reston, VA: ERIC Clearinghouse on Disabilities and Gifted Children.

Boehnlein, M. (1987). Reading intervention for high-risk first-graders. *Educational Leadership*, March 1987, 32-37.

Ekwall, E. (1986). A teacher's handbook on diagnosis and remediation in reading (2nd edition). Boston: Alan & Bacon.

Frost, J., & Emery, M. (Spring 1996). Academic interventions for children with dyslexia who have phonological core deficits. *Teaching Exceptional Children*, 80-83.

Grossen, B., & Carnine, D. (1993). Phonics instruction: Comparing research and practice. *Teaching Exceptional Children, 25*(2), 22-25.

Haynes, M.C., & Jenkins, J. (1986). Reading instruction in special education resource rooms. *American Educational Research Journal, 23*(2), 161-190.

Hiebert, E.H. (Dec. 1994). Reading recovery in the United States: What difference does it make to an age cohort? *Educational Researcher*, 15- 25.

Jenkins, J., Jewell, M., Leicester, M., O'Connor, R., Jenkins, L., & Troutner, N. (1994). Accomodations for individual differences without classroom ability groups: An experiment in school restructuring. *Exceptional Children, 60*(4), 344-358.

Klinger, J.K., & Vaughn, S. (1996). Reciprocal teaching of reading comprehension strategies for students with learning disabilities who use English as a second language. *Elementary School Journal, 96*(3), 275-293.

Lewis, R. (1983). Learning disabilities and reading: Instructional recommendations from current research. *Exceptional Children, 50*(3), 230-240.

Mandelbaum, L. (1989). Reading. In G. Robertson, J. Patton, E. Palloway, & L. Sargeant (EDS), *Best practices in mild mental retardation.* Reston, VA: The Division on Mental Retardation of the Council for Exceptional Children, 87-108.

McCormick, S. (1994). A nonreader becomes a reader: A case study of literacy acquisition by a severely disabled reader. *Reading Research Quarterly, 29*(2), 156-176.

Orlando, C. (1973). Review of the reading research in special education. In Mann, L., &Sabatino, D. *The first review of special education, Vol. 1.* Philadelphia: JSE Press, 261-283.

Orr, P.B. (1989). Improving critical reading skills by use of multiple methods/materials individualized instruction. ERIC document reproduction service ED323507.

Pinnell, G.S. (1989). Reading recovery: Helping at-risk children learn to read. *Elementary School Journal, 90*(2), 161-183.

Pinnell, G.S. (1990). Success for low achievers through reading recovery. *Educational Leadership, 48*, 17-21.

Rieth, H.J., Polsgrove, L., Raiq, S., Patterson, H., & Brichman, K. (1977). The use of free time to increase the reading achievement of three students placed in programs for behavior disordered children. *Behavior Disorders, 3*, 45-54.

Ross, S.M., Smith, L.J., Casey, J., & Slavin, R.E. (1995). Increasing the academic success of disadvantaged children: An examination of alternative early intervention programs. *American Educational Research Journal, 32*(4), 773-800.

Saski, J., & Carter, J. (1984). Effective reading instruction for mildly handicapped adolescents. *Teaching Exceptional Children, 16*(3), 177-182.

Stephans, M.A. (1993). Developing and implementing a curriculum and instructional program to improve reading achievement of middle grade students with learning disabilities in a rural school district. ERIC Document Reproduction Service ED 359492.

Swanson, L. (1981). Modification of comprehension deficits in learning disabled children. *Learning Disability Quarterly, 4*, 189-202.

Yoshimoto, R. (1997). Phonemes, phonetics, and phonograms: Advanced language structures for students with learning disabilities. *Teaching Exceptional Children, 29*, 43-48.

Chapter 8

MATHEMATICS

Many children with educational handicaps not only have trouble with language and reading skills, but also with mathematics as well. In fact, problems in mathematics are second only to those in reading for educationally handicapped children.

There are a variety of specific strategies teachers can employ to facilitate the learning of mathematics facts and concepts (McDougall and Brady, 1998). One method that has been used successfully in the area of mathematics is the use of **mnemonics**. Mnemonics are, simply put, strategies designed to aid the memory in recalling information. Mnemonics have been in use by teachers for many years, but it is only recently that their use has been tied directly to assisting educationally handicapped children. An example of a mnemonic strategy would be to employ the acronym "HOMES" to remember the Great Lakes of the United States. The Great Lakes are Huron, Ontario, Michigan, Erie and Superior, and HOMES is what is known as an acronym mnemonic. An acronym is a word formed by the first letters of other words to facilitate recall of the desired words or concepts.

Acronyms are especially useful for educationally handicapped students because these students often lack the ability to recall information from their long term memory or to employ other metacognitive strategies to facilitate learning. Typically mathematics instruction proceeds from the concrete to the representational and finally to the abstract. At the concrete level students are exposed to manipulatives, and they can see and feel and actually manipulate the materials with which they are working. When competency level has been achieved, teachers typically move on to teach similar skills at the representational level. At this level pictures and other representational devices are employed. Finally, the students are moved to working at the abstract level which allows only the use of numbers. Educationally handicapped students often succeed at mastering the concrete and sometimes the representational level but most have difficulty working at the abstract level. This is where acronym mnemonics can be helpful.

The following acronym can be used at a variety of grade levels to assist students in solving basic mathematical problems involving addition, subtraction, multiplication and division.

"SOLVE"

1. **See the sign**. What operation is called for? Is it addition, subtraction, multiplication or division.

2. **Observe and answer**. Look at the numbers involved and attempt to answer the problem.

3. **Look and draw**. If the student cannot answer he/she could be encouraged to graphically or with tally marks attempt to solve the problem

4. **Verify your answer**. Have the student go over the process ensure that his/her response is correct.

5. **Enter your answer**. Write the answer where it is called for.

Example: 9 x 5=

1.   The sign calls for multiplying.

2.   Student does not know the answer.

3. $9 + 9 + 9 + 9 + 9$ Tally the numbers to arrive at an answer.

4.   Review your strategies to assure that 45 is the correct answer.

5.   Write the answer 45 at the appropriate location.

"DRAW" is another acronym which is easy to employ.
1. **Discover the sign**. What operation is called for in the problem.

2. **Read the problem**. Read out loud or silently to reinforce what the problem is asking you to do.

3. **Answer or draw pictures or tally marks**. Answer the problem if you know it. If you do not know it draw a picture or tally marks to solve the problem.

4. **Write the answer where it is called for**. Both "SOLVE" and "DRAW" can be used to teach addition, subtraction, multiplication or division. Both can be used in the elementary grades although DRAW is better for primary students because it tends to be somewhat simpler than SOLVE.

These acronym mnemonics are particularly helpful in aiding educationally handicapped students with mathematical word problems. Word problems tend to be particularly troublesome for these students because they often have difficulty determining what information is important and necessary to solve the problem and what information is not essential. Also, the task is complicated by the fact that educationally handicapped students often have difficulty in reading as well as in mathematics.

MATH TEACHING STRATEGIES

Mathematics remediation for educationally handicapped students often begins with basic mathematical facts and operations. However, many of these students have difficulty maintaining and generalizing these skills after acquisition. Math skills can be practiced by using textbooks or worksheets; however, "since this group of learners has difficulty with generalizations, bringing mathematics experiences into the home assists in their development of generalization skills" (Bruneau, 1988, p. 16). Use of mathematics skills in the home involves the parent in the important role of helping their child reinforce school learning. These skills also assist the educationally handicapped student to prepare for real-life experiences which require the use of mathematics. By teaching through real-life experiences, teachers and parents can "look for mathematics in the environment" (Bruneau, 1988, p. 17). Visiting the grocery store and practicing finding the price of an item, identifying coins, reading numbers on a license plate, on television or in the newspaper continually reinforce basic math skills.

Individualized math instruction is another teaching strategy useful for educationally handicapped students. Stainback, Stainback, and Stefanich (1996) advocate that basic educational goals for mildly educationally handicapped students remain the same as their nonhandicapped peers. However, the specific learning objectives may be individualized in some instances to fit skills, interests, abilities, and unique needs of the students. In an effort to individualize math instruction and enhance learning for these students, Plata and Calvin (1984) recommend the concept of "centers" for each Learning Activity Mini-Packet that could be developed for each math skill. These learning centers contain instructions for the activity and all materials needed to complete the objectives and skills.

Burke (1989) points out that manipulative materials have a high probability of producing improved mathematics achievement. These objects appeal to several senses and allow the student to touch, handle, and move them in an effort to understand basic math skills and to employ math concepts. Manipulative materials can be bought or hand-made. Commonly used manipulatives are counting devices, pattern shapes, geo boards, rulers, colored rods, number balances, play money, and clocks.

The best mathematic instructional materials for educationally handicapped students are "simple, have a clear purpose, are easily repetitive, and match as closely as possible the vocabulary and methods being used" (Vacc, 1995, p. 50). These criteria need to be met so as not to confuse these students. A useful manipulative, the hundreds chart, "is simple and repetitive in design and provides an excellent resource for addressing the different components of number sense" (Vacc, p. 50). To eliminate confusing educationally handicapped students, Vacc modified the hundreds chart to align its format with the vocabulary and methods used when manipulating numbers. It includes the numbers 0 to 99 and it progresses from right to left. "The right-to-left format of the restructured hundreds chart is aligned with (a) place value changes, which progress from right to left; and (b) addition, subtraction, and multiplication, all of which invlove sequential steps that process from right to left" (Vacc, 1995. p. 50).

Diagnostic or clinical teaching is a useful method for gathering information that will help all children learn, especially those who are educationally handicapped. In order to use this method, Fowler (1978) insists that teachers must consider first, exactly which error the child is making; second, what is the child's rationale for the error, and what does the child need to remediate the situation. In an effort to determine errors a student is making, "work space must be provided directly on the assignment sheets, and the teacher must instruct the students to use it for all their work, including scratch work" (Fowler, 1978, p. 24). Just a few examples of problems which can be analyzed through clinical teaching are the concept of zero, use of the number 1, practice of erroneous procedures, failure to check work, number of digits or symbols which confuse a student with disabilities, and the child misreading his own work due to poor penmanship.

THE LANGUAGE OF MATHEMATICS

Mathematical vocabulary typically used by educators needs to be simple and informal. Educationally handicapped students need to be able to understand and master a group of informal keywords used in most mathematics curricula. Teachers need to determine such words and continually reinforce them in their teaching even when mathematics textbooks use a more formal language. "The core of keywords from the textbooks emphasized mathematical terms (e.g. fraction, multiply), whereas the teacher's core of keywords suggested the use of ordinary words to explain the language of mathematics to the students" (Cawley & Parmar, 1990, p. 515).

Often students who are educationally handicapped experience frustration with math skills due to difficulties in executing written math processes. "Arithmetic computation is most often presented to mildly handicapped children via paper-and-pencil methods and rule-governed routines" (Cawley & Parmar, 1990, p. 517). For example, starting addition facts with the column on the right then carry numbers to the next column makes computation a burden for many students with disabilities. We need to take advantage of technology to facilitate the mathematics learning of educationally handicapped children. "Calculators and microcomputers need to become integral facets of the program" (Cawley & Parmar, 1990, p. 516).

With diverse groupings of students learning together in inclusive classrooms, math curriculum must be "adaptive, flexible, and challenging to all students" (Stainback, Stainback, & Stefanich, 1996, p.

14). General educators, instruction specialists, and other specialists must collaborate to adapt activities in an effort to pursue different objectives for students. Students could be included by various means from their use of similar but different worksheets, to practice number recognition, to "a class activity to provide all the students participation in a practical real-life experience in applying what they had been learning in the math class" (Stainback, Stainback, & Stefanich, 1996, p. 16).

TEACHING MATH IN INTEGRATED SETTINGS

A majority of educationally handicapped students are, and more will be, educated in the regular classroom. Plata and Cavin (1984) state that most regular class teachers are ill-equipped to handle the trauma caused by the "invasion" of atypical pupils on existing traditional classroom routines. In an effort to establish individualized instruction needed for these students, curriculum specialists, special educators and regular classroom teachers must "develop specific competencies to individualize education, especially at the elementary level where basic academic skills are emphasized" (Plata & Cavin, 1984, p. 131). For the mildly educationally handicapped, "their cognitive abilities and ability to utilize mathematics concepts and principles would be better met by a substantially reduced emphasis on arithmetic computation and an expanded emphasis on mathematics in contextual settings that emulates the everyday world" (Cawley & Parmar, 1990, p. 510).

Burke (1989) points out that:

> Although manipulative materials were available in the classrooms, most did not receive frequent use. When manipulatives were used, it was primarily in ways that could be incorporated into a traditional, deductive skills- or fact-oriented curriculum rather than for developing mathematical concepts for problem-solving, or inquiry, which is a basis for the educationally handicapped mathematics program (p. 13).

Mathematical curriculum for mildly educationally handicapped students is centering more around individualized and small group instruction. The use of clinical teaching would be greatly beneficial in determining instructional group levels. However, "many teacher-training institutions evidently do not incorporate this topic in their curricula" (Fowler, 1978, p. 25).

Teaching mathematics to the mildly educationally handicapped is further complicated for teachers by textbook publishers. In an effort to teach curriculum, teachers rely on related textbooks. However, "publishers do not consider curriculum adjustments for handicapped students when preparing their materials" (Cawley & Parmar, 1990, p. 507). Textbooks are consistent and expect that students generally work on the same assignment in the same manner with fixed frequency of repetitions. Educationally handicapped students need repetition and practice to assure mastery and generalization of mathematical skills. Also, textbooks may be difficult for many educationally handicapped students to read. "If the area of discrepancy is reading, the child might receive less than the measure of a mathematics lesson because he or she might not be able to read the text" (Cawley & Parmar, 1990, p. 511). During his research Burke (1989) also found that most commercial texts were visually confusing for mildly educationally handicapped students.

There is no question that educationally handicapped students need to learn math skills. Different teaching strategies and curriculum modifications must be used in an effort to assist to develop math activities that are "informal and fun and help develop a positive feeling toward mathematics" (Bruneau, 1988, p. 16). Educators, whether special or regular classroom teachers, need to adapt their mathematical language to be more informal so students with disabilities can understand key words. Also, textbook publishers must be more adapted to the mathematical language needed by these students. Manipulative materials need to not only be located in classrooms, but need to be frequently used in order for the mildly educationally handicapped to develop, understand, and practice basic math skills. Manipulatives also help develop problem solving concepts. Positive results have been experienced by these students when using the restructured hundreds chart. This chart helps to develop math activities for students with disabilities "at a more abstract level than other manipulatives" (Vacc, 1995, p. 55). Restructured hundreds charts "can help students with disabilities construct mathematical meanings and develop a better understanding of number sense" (Vacc, 1995, p. 55). Diagnostic teaching helps the teacher understand "the student's thinking process" (Fowler, 1978, p.

24) and modify teaching strategies and curriculum material to the needs of the mildly educationally handicapped. Small group learning, individualized instruction centers, and practice of basic math skills used in the environment help the mildly educationally handicapped utilize mathematics. Through the use of these techniques they also learn to use math in problem solving. Teaching strategies in the mathematics curriculum for mildly educationally handicapped students "must focus on mathematical reasoning, understanding, and the ability to apply computation in real-life situations" (Cawley & Parmar, 1990, p. 518).

INFORMAL ASSESSMENT ACTIVITY
Scenairo:

Harold is struggling with word problems in his fourth grade math class. He has always excelled at math—easily grasping mathematics concepts, numeration, and operational procedures. In fact, math is one of Harold's favorite subjects. At least, it has been up until now.

Since the start of the unit focusing on word problems, Harold's mathematics performance has changed dramatically. Whereas he used to be the first person in the class to volunteer to work out the problems on the board, he no longer participates or shows much enthusiasm for the subject matter. In addition, his assignments are either unfinished or filled with errors.

Even though he has shown mastery over more basic mathematical problems such as simple computations, the teacher to make certain that these skills are still intact. By doing this the teacher can determine if perhaps the problem lies in the actual computation and not the word problem. The teacher prepares a review lesson, in the form of a mathematical probe, to be given to the entire class on various addition, subtraction, multiplication, and division problems that had been covered in previous units.

The students are given a ten minute, in-class "see-write" exercise. The teacher determines that students should achieve a 50-80 answer per minute fluency rate for addition and subtraction problems, and a 40-50 answer per minute rate for multiplication and division problems. The results of the probe confirm Harold's fluency in computation.

Next, the teacher readdresses the subject of word problems, but keeps them simple and direct, without any excess information. On a worksheet, the class has been asked to attempt the following problem:

James has twice as many baseball cards as Mark.
Mark has twelve baseball cards. How many baseball
cards does James have? ($12 \times 2 = 24$)

Harold is able to solve this kind of word problem easily, so a more
difficult problem is presented:

Two buses leave a terminal at the same time and travel
in opposite directions. One bus travels at 55 mi/hr. The
other travels at 48 mi/hr. A third bus leaves the terminal
headed for Boston at 60 mi/hr. How far apart will the
buses be in 3 hours?

In this instance, Harold is unable to determine what computation is
needed with what information to get the correct answer. The teacher
introduces the "SOLVE" acronym mnemonic to the whole class to see
if this will help Harold. The mnemonic device I choose to use is
"SOLVE."
Mnemonic devices can be taught in a creative way, using flashcards,
games, or even cooperative learning groups, making it more appealing to the students. Once Harold and all the other students learn what
"SOLVE" stands for and how to apply it to a word problem, the class
is asked to try a few problems, including the one about the buses.
    1. **See the problem:** (read the problem)
    2. **Observe and organize the facts:** There are really only two
buses to be concerned about. (The ones leaving at the same time).
They are travelling away from each other, so they will be far apart in
3 hours. One is travelling 55 mph for 3 hrs. while the other is travelling 48 mph for 3 hours.
    3. **Line up a plan:** First, I need to figure out how many miles each
bus will have travelled after 3 hours. Then I need to find out how far
apart, in miles, they will be after 3 hours.
    4. **Verify your plan with computation:**
    Bus#1: $55 \times 3 = 165$ miles after 3 hrs.
    Bus #2: $48 \times 3 = 144$ miles after 3 hrs.
    $165 + 144 = 309$ miles apart after 3 hrs.
    5. **Enter your answer:** Does this make sense? Yes, because the
buses are travelling away from each other, therefore the answer should
be a somewhat large number.

Harold's use of the "SOLVE" mnemonic provides the added skills he may need to obtain the correct answer to word problems.

REFERENCES

Bruneau, O.J. (1988). Involving parents in the mathematics education of their young handicapped child. *Arithmetic Teacher, 36,* 16-18.

Burke, J.P. (1989). Implementing a manipulative, Piagetian mathematics curriculum for primary, educationally handicapped pupils. Ed.D. Practicum, Nova University ERIC document reproduction service ED 313863.

Cawley, J.F., & Parmar, R.S. (1990). Issues in mathematics curriculum for handicapped students. *Academic Therapy, 25,* 507-521.

Fowler, M.A. (1978). Why did he miss that problem? *Academic Therapy, 14,* 23 - 33.

McDougall, D., & Brady, M. (1998). Initiating and fading self-management interventions to increase math fluency in general education classes. *Exceptional Children, 64* (2), 151-166.

Plata, M., & Cavin, J. (1984). Number skill development in mainstreamed handicapped students. *Teaching Exceptional Children, 40,* 131-135.

Riegel, R.H. (1974). Teaching potentially educationally handicapped children to classify and remember. *Exceptional Children, 40,* 208-209.

Stainback, W., Stainback, S., & Stefanich, G. (1996). Learning together in inclusive classrooms. *Teaching Exceptional Children, 28,* 14-19.

Tozloski, J.H. (1995). Making math fun! Teaming and creative scheduling is the key. *Schools in the Middle, 5,* 10-12.

Vacc, N. Gaining number sense through a restructured hundreds chart. *Academic Therapy, 25,* 507-521.

Chapter 9

MANAGING THE TEACHING AND LEARNING ENVIRONMENT

It has hopefully been established that individualizing instruction requires the use of assessment information, and that an individualized remedial plan cannot be successfully initiated without the use of teacher-collected assessment information. Once sufficient assessment information has been gathered, it is appropriate to formulate instructional objectives for each student. These instructional objectives must be specified as specific tasks the learner is expected to accomplish. As the educationally handicapped learners begin to perform these tasks, it is frequently necessary to engage in task analysis, because it is not unusual to find that educationally handicapped learners are often unsuccessful or partially successful in the specific task. This requires the analysis of the tasks in an attempt to pinpoint some skills that the students have difficulty performing. By engaging in this task analysis, the teacher is identifying the specific problems that the child is having, and simultaneously formulating new or modified instructional objectives.

Consideration has also been given to how to sequence the specific instructional tasks in a logical manner and assist the educationally handicapped child through this task hierarchy. The primary method of instruction in remedial instruction is of course direct instruction. This topic was addressed in Chapter 4, and in the course of providing direct instruction, it is essential that the teacher or the learning facilitator learn to provide immediate feedback to the learner on his performance. In other words, mistakes should be corrected immediately and correct responses should be reinforced immediately. The immediacy of these activities cannot be stressed too heavily.

MANAGING THE LEARNING ENVIRONMENT

In order to successfully perform the teaching activities specified above and in order to maximize the educationally handicapped learner's opportunity to succeed, it is essential to structure and manage the environment in which the specified tasks are being performed. In summarizing the literature on the instructional contexts learning disabled students experience, Rose and Rose (1994) point out that studies of teacher behavior have shown that teachers in regular classrooms respond more frequently and negatively to off-task behavior by learning disabled students than to that of other students. They also tend to direct fewer academic questions and less extended feedback to learning disabled students than to their nonlearning disabled classmates. Macintosh, et al. (1993) substantiated that learning disabled students interacted with the teacher, with other students, and in classroom activities at a much lower rate than a general education student. This finding was supported in a study conducted by Fox (1989).

Nevertheless, if the special education environment is carefully managed, the likelihood of success on learning tasks increases, and it is increasingly probable that the learner may be returned full-time to the regular classroom. Scruggs and Mastropieri (1992) contend that in order to be effectively mainstreamed, students must function effectively within the following eight general areas:

1. **attention**–Attention has long been identified as a major prerequisite for school learning.

2. **memory**–Short-term memory, long-term memory, and the use of efficient memory strategies.

3. **intellectual abilities**–General intellectual deficits are frequently used to identify mentally retarded students; however, less pronounced deficits in intellectual functioning have been identified in learning disabled and seriously emotionally disturbed students.

4. **language**–Language problems including receptive and expressive language problems are typical characteristics of educationally handicapped children.

5. **social/behavioral characteristics**–Including disruptive behavior, withdrawal, aggression, interpersonal skills, cultural/language differences and general social skills.

6. **affective/motivational factors**–Often a problem with educationally handicapped children due to history of school failure.

7. **basic academic skills**–One of the most fundamental character-istics of handicapped children.

8. **study/organizational skills**–Includes listening, note-taking, study strategies, research and composition skills, and test-taking skills. (390)

These topics, important to remedial instruction, will be addressed later in this chapter.

MOTIVATION

Student motivation is an important consideration in remedial edu-cation. Motivation is a term that is frequently misused because some educators see it exclusively as a hypothetical construct rather than as a variable that can be operationally defined. We often hear statements like "She just isn't motivated," suggesting that this internal factor, rather than the teaching/learning ecology, is preventing her from being successful. Because the topic can be confusing, it is important to think about motivation in at least two different ways.

The way most educators with a strong behavioral orientation tend to think about motivation is to divide it into extrinsic and intrinsic cat-egories. Extrinsic motivation comes from outside the learner; it can be thought of as reinforcement. There are external variables which are reinforcing enough that when delivered to the learner serve as a form of extrinsic motivation. In other words, the child is motivated to engage in the desired behavior because of the potential of the extrin-sic reinforcer. Intrinsic motivation, on the other hand, is a type of motivation which is internal to the child. It is the type of motivation that we like to see in all children, but unfortunately, it does not exist in all children, especially those with educational handicaps. Rose and Rose (1994) contend that recent research on motivation and achieve-ment-related behavior has demonstrated the importance of students' perceptions of and beliefs about their competence as learners, about their control over their own success and failure, and about the tasks expected of them in school. They go on to suggest that a considerable amount of evidence shows that such beliefs largely determine the degree of effort students will expend in learning activities and the strategies they will employ to achieve academic goals. They conclude that this may be particularly important for learning disabled students who are frequently described as passive or disassociated learners who tend not to participate heavily in the learning process. The goal, of course, is to build intrinsic motivation in each and every educationally handicapped learner. When a child develops a natural curiosity, a willingness to participate, and a desire to achieve, it can be said that she has developed intrinsic motivation.

It is also possible to consider motivation in another way. It may be also be helpful to think of motivation as general motivation or specific motivation. General motivation is somewhat equivalent to intrinsic motivation. That is, the source of the motivation is the learner, and it tends to be stable over time. Some students are generally motivated; they are interested in most topics and are willing participants in the teaching/learning environment. The other type of motivation is specific motivation. In this case, the source of this motivation is the teacher or the topic of instruction. It tends to be unstable and depends upon the particular situation. In remedial education it is important to stress specific motivation. Teachers need to be sensitive to the requirement of making the topic as interesting and appealing as possible. In the long run, success on specific tasks will assist in developing the more stable general motivation (i.e., interested, willing participants in the learning process).

CLASSROOM MANAGEMENT OR DISCIPLINE

Because of frustration and lack of academic success, educationally handicapped students occasionally cause discipline or other classroom management problems. There are several strategies which can be employed to improve discipline and to create an environment of order. For example, a shrewd teacher can employ several management strategies which require no speaking on the part of the teacher. Most educators are aware of the teacher who can give a significant glance or stare and successfully bring that student back to task. Occasionally it is appropriate for a teacher to move herself to the general area of the student who is misbehaving. Simply by moving into the proximity of the student, the student often returns to task. Sometimes teachers can avoid potential discipline problems by removing physical objects which are causing the disruption or off-task behavior. For example, removing a comic book from off-task students without comment is an appropriate classroom strategy and often brings the children back to task without further disruption. The most difficult thing for a teacher to do is to learn to **ignore** inappropriate behavior. This strategy, in the long run, is extremely effective and should be employed when possible. Ignored behavior is likely to extinguish, and as long as the off-task behavior is not harmful or terribly disruptive to other students, it is a good idea to ignore it and reinforce the first occurrence of appropriate behavior.

The most important aspect of classroom management is **consistency**. It is necessary to have rules and it is essential to consistently enforce the rules of the classroom. Most discipline problems are alleviated by careful planning. If the lessons are interesting and if the students know there is a certain order to the day or the period, many discipline problems can be avoided.

Discipline problems or other inappropriate behavior are in fact forms of antisocial or asocial behavior. Consequently, it is important to consider the development of social skills in educationally handicapped children. Scruggs and Mastropieri (1992) state that in terms of social/emotional behavior, it is of course imperative to reinforce positive classroom behavior. In order to make this easier, it is helpful to operationalize or describe behaviors in ways that are easily observable. As an example, the passage of an interval of time in which a student does not disrupt should be followed immediately by an appropriate positive reinforcer. Sometimes, peer mediation or the involvement of school district support personnel are appropriate to create improvement in this area. Perhaps most importantly is the admonition to directly teach social skills or appropriate behaviors when they are lacking. Student motivation for such activities will be enhanced if you have created a positive caring atmosphere in the classroom.

Cullinan et al. (1992) point out teachers' efforts to improve social behaviors are facilitated by categorizing social problems as skills deficits (student does not possess a skill), performance deficits (student does not perform skill appropriately), or behavior excess (student over-performs a skill). They suggest that social skills can be effectively taught by adhering to the following plan:

• make inventory of key social skills necessary for success in the given environment

- assess the handicapped student on these skills
- describe the social behavior to be taught
- demonstrate the behavior
- have student immediately demonstrate the behavior
- provide feedback
- provide naturalistic practice.
- phase out planned practice and feedback over time (p. 342)

In discussing atypical learners, Torrey et al. (1992) state "the acquisition of social skills has become as important to success in school and other environments as the acquisition of academic skills" (248). In terms of teaching or training social skills, they maintain that current curricula do not adequately address problems of producing behavioral changes that actually make handicapped youngsters more socially acceptable. In their study, Torrey et al. (1992) used four dependent measures: sociometric peer nominations, Social Skills Rating Skill-Teacher, Piers Harris Self-Concept Scale, and behavioral ratings as indications of students' social skills. They point out: "Social skills training generated improvement in both pre/postmeasures in behavioral ratings. Increased ratings were maintained two weeks after treatment was discontinued for the seven subjects. Improvement in all subjects' ratings generalized from resource room to regular classroom settings..." (252). "Perhaps the most striking finding in the present study was generalization from the resource room training setting to the non-training regular classroom setting" (253).

There can be little argument that social skill development is vitally important to educationally handicapped children. Cullinan et al (1992) point out that the social problems of the mildly handicapped must not go unaddressed. They may lead to an increase in dropping out or grade repeating, and later to juvenile delinquency and psychological adjustment problems. The more that an educationally handicapped child is socially integrated, the more successful will be the entire mainstreaming experience. Socially integrated is defined by Cullinan et al. (1992) as a child who is socially accepted by peers, has at least one reciprocal friendship, and is an equal participant in activities performed by peers. Mildly handicapped students are usually socially rejected, unpopular, and unwanted as classmates, workmates, and playmates because of inappropriate behavior that they exhibit.

In summarizing the literature concerning the acceptance of learning disabled children by nonhandicapped children, Fox (1989) concludes that previous research has shown that mainstreaming will not automatically help handicapped children become socially accepted by nonhandicapped peers, that there is sufficient evidence to demonstrate that disabled children are more often socially rejected by their non-handicapped peers than are non-handicapped children, and that mainstreaming by itself may not be enough to ensure the social acceptance of handicapped children.

Smith et al. (1994) have demonstrated that students with established patterns of exhibiting anger and aggression can be taught to control that behavior through cognitive-behavioral training. Teaching educationally handicapped children to engage in appropriate behavior could well be a very important aspect of a meaningful working definition of "effective discipline" and "social skills development."

ORGANIZATION OF INSTRUCTION

In order for an educationally handicapped student to learn effectively, she must attend to the teacher and the task, remember information efficiently, think clearly and logically, and employ language appropriately.

To improve an educationally handicapped student's **attention**, Scruggs and Mastropieri (1992) suggest modifying the rate that the curriculum is being presented. Sometimes teachers move too quickly for students to maintain attention. Another suggestion was to speak to a student privately about the importance of paying attention in class. Often, increasing a student's attention can be achieved by moving into a position more proximate to the student during instruction. Certainly, strategies should be employed to allow for the direct immediate reinforcement of attending behavior.

In terms of improving the **memory** skills of educationally handicapped children, teachers can intensify the instruction. This can sometimes be achieved by highlighting important points on the chalkboard or on the overhead. It is always a good idea to have students repeat the information back to the teacher. The teacher's use of direct questioning and guided rehearsal can also enhance memory. Additionally, the use of mnemonic devices is a good way of helping students improve their memory. Lastly, they suggest that a strategy for the effective improvement of memory is the direct active participation of the student in the learning process.

When addressing **intellectual deficits**, Scruggs and Mastropieri (1992) observe that it is important to make the material being presented as meaningful to the learner as possible. One suggestion to accomplish this would be to try to relate the student's direct experience to the content being studied. Secondly, they suggest that it is appropriate to provide additional time for children with intellectual deficits to achieve criterion. Teachers should pay close attention to the developmental level of the material. Often, instructional materials at a particular grade level are not appropriate in terms of the interest in the content to children with a higher chronological age.

Language skills are among the most important skills for educationally handicapped children to develop. As a series of strategies for developing these skills, Scruggs and Mastropieri (1992) recommend:

1. Allow the student sufficient time to respond—it is not uncommon for such students to have expressive language problems and they may simply require additional time
2. Assist students in developing listening skills—help students understand the important times for attending and then periodically check their understanding
3. Integrate language into regular instruction
4. Encourage and support special services in language training.

As Scruggs and Mastropieri (1992) point out, "A major cause of mainstreaming failure is a lack of **basic skills**, such as reading, writing, and math skills" (p. 401). The more serious the lack of basic skills, the more likely this problem should be addressed in the special education setting. Otherwise, direct teaching in the regular classroom is the most important way to improve basic skills. In addition to the direct instruction of the skills, it is helpful to (if appropriate) use parents as tutors, use appropriate peers as tutors, and to employ cooperative learning strategies. This being said, it is nonetheless important to directly teach that effort rather than luck is related to academic success. Sometimes having a successful student explain to the educationally handicapped student how she studies or prepares for a test or assignment can be quite helpful.

Finally, in terms of **study skills**, it is important to provide structure for educationally handicapped students. Teachers should be very explicit with all assignments and if possible models of appropriately completed assignments. All requirements for each assignment or project should be explicitly provided and repeated. This includes timelines and due dates. It is also wise to directly teach general study techniques. For example, educationally handicapped students should be taught the best ways to preview and review reading material, to take notes on class discussions and lectures, and highlighting and outlining procedures and general organizational skills concerning notebooks, textbooks, and other study materials. In addition, educationally handicapped children can be helped by directly teaching them particular test formats. For example, a teacher might want to prepare them for the types of evaluation that a teacher will employ by providing sample questions or practice tests.

SELECTING INSTRUCTIONAL MATERIALS

The instructional materials used by teachers to teach educationally handicapped children constitute an important topic and require careful consideration and reflection. Simmons et al. (1991) attempt to highlight specific insufficiencies of commercial curricula for instructionally needy students and also discuss the limitations of generic instructional procedures in addressing the needs of students with learning problems. Commercially available developmental curricula are the primary medium of instruction in the majority of special and mainstreamed classrooms. In large measure these commercial materials determine what is taught, as well as how it is taught. Consequently, serious consideration should be given to evaluating the appropriateness of such curricula for the mainstreamed educationally handicapped child.

The target audience that dictates the content and design of the developmental curricula is the normally achieving student. While these curricula may be appropriate in such cases, they are often inadequate for educationally handicapped learners. Gross generalizations about sequences of instruction and about time needed and practice required for heterogeneous groups of learners may be inappropriate when applied to students who require more or different instruction. The authors (Simmons et al., 1991) suggest that existing information shows that when students with handicaps are part of the academic mainstream, instruction is largely undifferentiated, directed to the whole class and driven by the text.

In addition, when planning for mainstreamed reading instruction in which basal curricula programs were the primary instructional tool, teachers reported making no modifications in instructional strategies over a six-week period. The evidence is clear that teachers tend to rely heavily on commercially available curricular materials. It is equally clear that the demands of the mainstreamed instructional ecology (e.g., large numbers of educationally handicapped students, class size, heterogeneity) may constrain their ability to individualize commercially available curricula to the instructional needs of students with educational handicaps.

PLANNING FOR REMEDIAL INSTRUCTION

In addition to determining the curriculum (that is identifying the objectives the student is expected to accomplish), methodology (how the teacher will assist the student accomplishing the objectives), and the instructional materials that will be employed, it is important for the teacher of educationally handicapped children to consider other variables as well. For example, it is important to consider the variable of **time**. How much time should be allocated to a particular instructional activity or to a particular objective? It is imperative to keep in mind that any decisions made relative to time are subject to change. Not only could it be appropriate to change the amount of time each day that a teacher devotes to a particular objective, but it also could be appropriate to continually modify the total amount of time in a term that a teacher devotes to a particular objective.

In terms of planning for instruction, Simmons et al. (1991) contend that consideration must be given to factors prior to instruction, during instruction and after instruction. They point out that prior to instruction, teachers should consider three important elements:

1. Time allocated for instruction
2. The objective of the lesson
3. Review of the prerequisite skills.

They go on to suggest that during instruction, teachers should:

1. Frame the task by explaining to students what they are going to learn, how they will use it, and why it is important.

2. Directly model the skill they are presenting and attempt to model multiple examples.
3. Specify a guided practice phase of instruction in which they check understanding, monitor student performance, and provide corrective feedback.
4. Prepare learners for independent practice.

At the conclusion of instruction, teachers are encouraged to actively monitor student performance during independent practice and review the instructional objective at the end of the lesson and in future lessons. "The long-term goal of education is to establish instructional environments that allow each student to reach potential and become an educated, independently functioning adult" (Simmons et al., 1991, 359).

Another variable worthy of a teacher's planning is the **location** of instruction. Clearly a decision needs to be made about how much instructional time will be undertaken in the special education setting compared to the amount of time devoted to instruction in the regular education classroom. It is important to remember that in order for generalization to occur it would be appropriate to carry instruction over from the special education setting to the regular education setting. Finally, it is important to determine who will be providing the direct instruction. In some cases it will be the special education teacher; in other cases, it will be the classroom teacher; and yet in other situations it might be an instructional aide. It is also likely that some other support personnel, such as librarian or physical education teacher, could be employed for some aspects of direct instruction. A rather careful consideration of the management of the classroom environment has been provided by Stephens, et al. (1982) in which they address the actual physical layout of the classroom with specific areas of that classroom identified. They also address the issues of instructional time and the grouping of students.

Included in anticipating and planning for the inclusion of educationally handicapped children in the classroom is the very important consideration of the layout or **geography** of the classroom. The resource room and the regular classroom should consist of discrete areas which become discriminative stimuli for specified student behavior. For example, it is important to fundamentally have what would be called the task area, which would consist of a section of the room where each student has a work station. This would be used not only for large group teaching but for seat work and other individual learning activities. In addition, there should be a portion of the room set aside for small group instruction. The teacher may find that a corner of the room with chairs in a semicircle may serve this purpose. The only requirement is that it be flexible enough to accommodate small groups of different sizes. It is also helpful to have a particular area of the classroom set aside for teacher assessment. This often is most effectively accomplished by having a work station adjacent to the teacher's desk. In this way, the teacher can be working directly on assessment activities with a student and not disrupt the other students in the task area. Finally, there should be a reinforcing event area. That is a portion of the room where students who earn the privilege can go for free play, use of games, listening to music, or arts and crafts activities.

These areas of the classroom would be in addition to any designated learning centers the teacher chooses to employ.

REFERENCES

Cullinan, D., Sabormie, E., & Crossland, C.L. (1992). Social mainstreaming of mildly handicapped students. *The Elementary School Journal, 92* (3), 339-351.

Deutsch Smith, D., & Rivera, D.P. (1995). Discipline in special education and general education settings. *Focus on Exceptional Children, 27* (5), 1-14.

Fox, C.L. (1989). Peer acceptance of learning disabled students in the regular classroom. *Exceptional Children, 56* (1), 50-59.

Howard-Rose, D., & Rose, C. (1994). Students' adaptation to task environments in resource room and regular class settings. *The Journal of Special Education, 28* (1), 3-26.

Macintosh, R., Vaughn, S., Schumm, J.S., Haggert, E., & Lee, O. (1993). Observations of students with learning disabilities in general education classrooms. *Exceptional Children, 16* (3), 249-261.

Scruggs, T.E., & Mastropieri, M.A. (1992). Effective mainstreaming strategies for mildly handicapped students. *The Elementary School Journal, 92* (3), 389-409.

Smith, W.W., Siegel, E.M., O'Connor, A.M., & Thomas, S.B. (1994). Effects of cognitive-behavioral training on angry behavior and aggression of three elementary-aged students. *Behavioral Disorders, 19* (2), 126-135.

Simmons, D.C., Fuchs, D., & Fuchs, L.S. (1991). Instructional and curricular requisites of mainstreamed students with learning disabilities. *Journal of Learning Disabilities, 24* (6), 354-359.

Stephens, T.M., Blackhurst, A.E., & Maglioccala (1982). *Teaching mainstreamed students.* New York: John Wylie & Sons.

Torrey, G.K., Vasa, S.F., Maag, J.W., & Kramer, J.J. (1992). Social skills interventions across school settings: Case study reviews of students with mild disabilities. *Psychology in the Schools, 29,* 248-55.

Chapter 10

COLLABORATION

It is undeniable that as a result of many factors including PL94-142, IDEA, the Regular Education Initiative and a variety of conceptualizations of inclusion, regular education is playing a much more prominent role in the lives of educationally handicapped children. With this increasing role of general education comes the natural requirement that collaboration between regular education and special education increase, not only in frequency but also in effectiveness. Collaboration can be defined as working together as coequal partners to achieve shared decision making on a mutually defined problem. Collaboration in schools has, and will continue, to include the involvement of parents as well. In actuality, the collaborative process of the future will undoubtedly include special education teachers, regular education teachers, school administrators, parents, and the students themselves. It is important to recognize the need for and importance of all levels of collaboration.

Of particular importance to educationally handicapped children is the collaboration that must occur between regular education teachers and special education teachers. The amount and quality of this collaboration is crucial because these teachers are the direct learning facilitators of these children. At this level, collaboration should lead to coordinated and individualized instruction. It is also important that teachers collaborate with parents because parents not only have a genuine interest in the educational program their child is receiving, but also because they can provide invaluable information to the teachers as they engage in instructional planning.

NEED FOR COLLABORATION

The need for special and regular education collaboration is becoming increasingly clear and has been corroborated by Schumm et al. (1995), who concluded that youngsters with learning disabilities can have expectations about general education which include:

• Teachers are not likely to develop individualized lesson plans
• Elementary teachers are more likely to plan individual assignments and alternative materials than are secondary teachers
• Teachers see the special education teacher as a primary resource in planning for students with special needs. Teachers will check on students' understanding of concepts and will provide adaptations to facilitate learning for the whole class but not for individuals.

Schumm et al. (1995) also indicate that even though general education teachers tended to view the special education teacher as a valuable resource in planning for students with learning disabilities, it could be reasonably expected that general education and special education teachers would not communicate and collaborate frequently. Clearly the importance for individualizing instruction is evident, and this is especially true when educationally handicapped children are integrated into their regular class.

WHY COLLABORATE?

The integration of educationally handicapped children into the regular classroom is a vitally important consideration and one that obviously requires careful planning, especially instructional planning.

Fulwider (1994) concludes that the literature has shown:

1. Instructional modifications are necessary for learning disabled students placed in regular classes.
2. Collaboration between special education teachers and regular education teachers can assist regular education teachers in developing appropriate modifications and strategies for teaching students with learning disabilities
3. A collaboration model which focuses on individual students, rather than on categories of students, has been shown to be most successful.

Evidence does suggest that a climate for collaboration can be created and when it is encouraged, it can be effective. In a five-year study, Osborne et al. (1991) found that special education and regular education teachers interacted with increasing frequency and that teachers rated students, who were mainstreamed, higher in behavior related to academic competence. Osborne et al. (1991) state, "At endpoint, however, almost ninety percent of the teachers reported meeting at least monthly with classroom teachers. Throughout the study, between seventy-four percent and ninety percent of teachers rated these meetings as positive" (87).

Marston and Heistad (1994) explain the development of a collaborative services model of education in a school district. In order to meet this school district's goal of a collaborative inclusion model, they found it necessary:

a. For schools to provide instruction for students with disabilities in general education classrooms.
b. Within these general education classrooms, special and general education teachers would establish collaborative arrangements and plan inclusive instruction for students with disabilities.
c. Within these collaborative arrangements, special education teachers would either provide direct instruction to students with disabilities in general education settings or provide consultation to the general education teachers who had primary responsibility for instruction.

The development of this collaborative services model seemed to be effective. According to Marston and Heisted (1994), "At many sites special and regular education teachers began to 'team' frequently for instructional planning, teaching, and assessment responsibilities" (54).

Public Law 94-142 was the first federal law mandating the right to free public education for all children, and this law was subsequently fine-tuned by IDEA. The Regular Education Initiative (REI) of 1986, proposed by former Assistant Secretary of Education Madeleine Will, presented a philosophy of education that attempts to establish a single educational system placing the primary responsibility of education on the regular educators in the regular classroom. In the name of inclusion, many school districts have committed more visibly to the integration of educationally handicapped children in the regular classroom. These pieces of legislation and educational movements have resulted in a more integrated instructional model. The demographics of the children in our classrooms is rapidly changing because of the growing national belief that exceptional children are better served in regular classrooms. Today, there is a trend toward full mainstreaming of students with mild disabilities (Whittier & Hewit, 1993). This new direction will require general educators to work with special educators "to learn strategies for teaching both students with and without disabilities together" (Whittier & Hewit, 1993, p. 84). Collaborative consultation is an educational service increasingly used to assist regular and special educators in this effort (West & Cannon, 1988). This delivery system is designed to meet the needs of all children–typical or exceptional–by dissolving the dual educational system and replacing it with a unitary school system to effectively and appropriately educate all students (Davis, 1989). Systematic implementation of educational collaboration in school cultures will be of significant value to teachers, students, and the entire school culture.

COLLABORATIVE STRATEGIES

According to West and Idol (1993), "The conceptual bridge from school consultation to collaborative consultation to collaboration in the schools is an important one" (p. 678). Idol and West (1991) maintain that in order to initiate collaborative consultation within a school, the staff must first come together and reach a consensus on the operational definition of collaboration. Once an agreement is made on the operational definition of collaboration as it pertains to decision-making, planning, and problem-solving in reference to critical areas that need change in the school environment, the staff can proceed to decide how the changes will be implemented within their school culture.

Schools would do well to employ the collaborative process in implementing all types of changes in the school culture needed for the integration of educationally handicapped children into the regular classroom. Explaining the collaborative system for the development of school-based teams that implement change, West (1990) offers this definition:

Education collaboration is an interactive planning, decision-making, or problem-solving process involving two or more team members. The process consists of up to eight interrelated, progressive steps:

1. Goal setting
2. Data collection
3. Problem identification
4. Alternative solutions development
5. Action plan development
6. Action plan implementation
7. Evaluation/follow-up
8. Redesign.

"Team interactions throughout the process are characterized by: mutual respect, trust, and open communication; consideration of each issue of problem from an ecological perspective; consensual decision-making; pooling of personal resources and expertise; and joint ownership of the issue or problem being addressed. The outcomes of educational collaboration may focus on changes in knowledge, skills, attitudes, or behaviors at one or more of three levels: child, adult, or system" (West, 1990, p. 29).

In many schools, members of department- and grade-level instructional teams are expected to assume responsibility for the education of each student who attends the school. Therefore, teachers on these committees usually plan and teach in teams. This collaboration occurs for planning purposes only in some schools; in other schools it occurs for both planning and instruction. Teacher assistance teams utilize preventative measures for students at risk of failure or of dropping out of school. Effective teacher assistance teams employ a system that allows a teacher to request assistance regarding a problem, join the team, and together systematically attempt to solve the problem.

Collaborative teaching programs utilize "coordinated special and general education instructional planning and program implementation" (Idol & West, 1991, p. 78). Idol and West (1991) report that at least one resource/consulting teacher is on the staff and provides consultative services to regular teachers and students with special needs. The services are both indirect (provided to a regular educator who has a student with special needs enrolled in his or her class) and direct (provided directly to a special needs student). The professional who fills the role of resource/consulting teacher varies from school to school.

"The critical point, of course, is that in educational collaboration, no one individual is expected to be the expert with the answer. Quality intervention action plans are usually the result of the synergy generated by the pooling of collective expertise and resources of collaborative team members. This principle of role and functional reciprocity cannot be overemphasized as a critical element in a true collaborative relationship" (West & Idol, 1990, p. 29).

With collaborative school environments, teaching does not have to be and should not be an isolated event. West and Idol (1990) point out that the notion of reciprocity and mutuality encourages teachers to allow each other equal access to information and problem-solving opportunities, share the ownership of common problems and issues as professionals, and together generate and maintain enthusiasm for the desired outcomes.

COLLABORATION IN PRACTICE

Many schools and districts have already implemented successful collaborative programs, a good example of which is the Joshua Independent School District located near Fort Worth, Texas. During the spring of 1992, the regular kindergarten teachers and the special education teacher at Joshua Elementary School worked together to implement a program where all kindergarten children were taught in regular classrooms. Pull-out programs were only used in a few cases where mainstreaming was not beneficial to the students. In most cases, the special education teachers worked in the classroom alongside the regular teacher (Young, 1993). For instance, the special education staff assisted the regular education staff by conducting small group lessons during certain instructional times in the classroom learning centers. Any students (special and regular) who needed help came to these small groups. The special education staff reviewed and retaught skills that were presented by the regular education teacher during lesson time (Young, 1993). Also, additional roles of special education teachers included team teaching, conducting small group review sessions, and redirecting off-task behavior when the regular teacher was teaching a lesson (Young, 1993).

As members of the team, special and regular educators take on additional and/or dual roles, and work cooperatively for the benefit of educationally handicapped children. For instance, special educators support regular teachers by providing necessary information about each child's needs and capabilities. They also offer regular teachers alternative methods for teaching and socializing the educationally handicapped student(s) in the regular classroom. "The special educators at Joshua Elementary are required to be flexible, in that they give up their own classrooms to work in the classrooms of other teachers. However, regular teachers also relinquish control and independence by allowing the special education teacher to share responsibility for the planning and teaching of students" (Young, 1993, p. 241).

The success of the collaborative program at Joshua Elementary School has been evaluated through interviews with parents, teachers, and administrators. The program has proven to be very successful, especially for the educationally handicapped child. "Another measure of success is that students who have participated in this program have continued to be placed in less restrictive environments" (Young, 1993, p. 242).

Also, in the two years the program has been in effect, there has been an increase in achievement scores in all areas which include receptive language, expressive language, auditory discrimination, visual memory, fine motor skills, and gross motor skills. Most notable increases have occurred in receptive language where some students have improved scores by two years (Young, 1993).

Looking at the overall collaborative program at Joshua Elementary School, it can be concluded that in general, disabled children have benefitted from being in a regular class where there are peers to model behavior and expectations for academic performance are higher (Young, 1993).

COLLABORATION WITH PARENTS

In addition to collaborating with each other, it is important for special education and regular education teachers to collaborate regularly with parents. Not only can parents offer insights into a child's performance which are routinely unavailable to teachers, but their legitimate involvement increases the likelihood of their actively supporting the educational program designed for their child.

Goldstein (1993) suggests that parents are often understandably intimidated by the prospect of an IEP conference or some other formal meeting with school personnel. Because the goal is to have parents become fully participating partners in the planning process, Goldstein (1993) offers the following suggestions for encouraging parent involvement:

- Contact parents personally before the meeting.
- Have a school staff member greet the parents.
- Avoid eating during conference.
- Appoint an interpreter.

"If the IEP is to succeed in facilitating development of an effective education program, parents must understand and be ready to undertake some responsibility for that program" (p. 61). It is important for teachers to work diligently to include parents in the process of designing the educational programs for their children.

Facilitating the Collaborative Process

What follows are some suggestions for teachers for proactively including parents in the collaborative process.

Suggestions for teachers in the collaborative process:

1. Realize some parents are distrustful of schools because their children have not been accepted or learned acceptably. Thus interactions with these parents can be difficult.

2. Inform yourself about community resources and give this information to parents. Be candid with parents about limitations in services.

3. Remember to keep communication open. (It's a two-way street with parents and teachers.) Allow parents to observe how you interact with the child and how you work. Then encourage them to practice this at home.

4. Make the parent a team member/partner in the actual diagnosis, treatment, or educational procedures. Encourage parents to help with teaching at home by helping with homework.

5. Be sure the parent understands no diagnosis is final. Explain why a label is given to a child and its repercussions. Also, caution against using it to explain a child's condition to other people.

6. Write reports in clear and understandable language so as not to confuse the parent or make it hard to understand.

7. Offer to parents copies of child's work, copies of your written comments on the work, and copies of any reports prepared or received about the child. Be sure the parent understands his child's abilities and assets as well as his disabilities and deficiencies.

Parents must also take some responsibility for assuring the success of the process of collaborating with teachers. What follows are some suggestions for parents:

Suggestions for parents in the collaborative process:

1. Assume an active rather than a passive role. Be a part of making the management plan, implementing it, determining its effectiveness and modifying it, if needed.

2. Be involved in every step of assessing the child's needs, but realize the teacher has the key role in all matters relating to the child's schooling.

3. Become a partner with the teacher. Observe how the teacher interacts with the child and how the teacher works. Then adapt this to what you do with your child at home.

4. Encourage and guide your child's instruction. Help your child with homework. Don't just supervise, but get involved.

5. Understand a "diagnosis" is never final. Understand why a label is given and its repercussions. Use caution not to use the label to explain the child's condition to other people.

6. Be sure you understand your child's abilities and assets as well as his disabilities and deficiencies.

7. Insist on being a part of all decisions about your child.

It is not only the educationally handicapped child who will benefit from collaborative consultation. Through collaboration, teachers learn how to communicate effectively within their work environment and how to utilize and offer professional support for service delivery in the form of individualized instruction to meet the needs of all students. The school is often improved because of effective communication between faculty, staff, and administrators; the teaching profession is advanced because of cooperative professional support; parents feel like they are playing a meaningful role in the education of their children; and all students benefit from individualized instruction as a result of these efforts.

REFERENCES

Davis, W. (1989). The regular education initiative debate: Its promise and problems. *Exceptional Children, 55,* 440-446.

Fulwider, N.A. (1994). Assisting regular education classroom teachers of elementary learning disabled students through collaboration. Ed.D. Practicum Report, Nova South Eastern University.

Goldstein, S. (1993). The IEP conference: Little things mean a lot. *Teaching Exceptional Children, 26*(1), 60-61.

Haager, D., McDowell, J., Rothlein, L., Saumell, L., & Schumm, J.S. (1995). General education teacher planning: What can students with learning disabilities expect? *Exceptional Children, 61*(4), 335-352.

Idol, L., & West, J.F. (1991). Educational collaboration: A catalyst for effective schooling. *Remedial and Special Education, 11*(1), 22-31.

Marston, D., & Heistad, D. (1994). Assessing collaborative inclusion as an effective model for the delivery of special education services. *Diagnostique, 9,* 451-467.

Osborne, S.S., Schulte, A.C., & McKinney, J.D. (1991). A longitudinal study of students with learning disabilities in mainstream and resource programs. *Exceptionality, 2*(2), 81-95.

West, J. F. (1990). Educational collaboration in the restructuring of schools. *Journal of Educational and Psychological Consultation, 1*(1), 23-40.

West, J.F., & Cannon, G.S. (1988). Essential collaborative consultation competencies for regular and special educators. *Journal of Learning Disabilities, 21*(1), 56-63, 28.

West, J.F., & Idol, L. (1990). Collaborative consultation in the education of mildly handicapped and at-risk students. *Remedial and Special Education, 11*(1), 22-31.

West, J.F., & Idol, L. (1993). The counselor as consultant in the collaborative school. *Journal of Consulting and Development, 71,* 678-683.

Young, E. (1993). *Engineering the classroom to promote inclusion.* Joshua, Texas: Joshua Independent School District. (ERIC Document Reproduction Service No. ED 369 614)

Appendix A

LITERACY RESOURCES FOR
EDUCATIONALLY HANDICAPPED STUDENTS

READING RESOURCES

Comprehension Power
Milliken Publishing Company
1100 Research Boulevard
P.O. Box 21579
St. Louis, Missouri 63132-0579

The main feature of the program is that it is designed to build reading comprehension in students. The program is equipped with various stories that cover a wide range of topics, such as sports, adventures and future careers that will appeal to boys and girls alike. The wide range of topics will allow a child to choose a topic and will maintain their interest. As a child becomes better at reading, he can move to increasingly higher levels with each level offering stories of increasing rigor.

A child can choose how much she wants to read at a time. She can choose to read one sentence at a time or can choose to read an entire page at a time. She has the ability to review an area as many times as she likes, until he is ready to move on. At the end of a reading segment, the child answers reading comprehension questions. The correct answer is displayed with pertinent information, if the child chooses an incorrect answer. Immediate feedback and positive reinforcement is provided if the child gives a correct answer. The program gives the child an overall summary of their performance at the end of each activity.

Cloze-Plus
Milliken Publishing Company
1100 Research Boulevard
P.O. Box 21579
St. Louis, Missouri 63132-0579

The main feature of this program is that it allows children to develop reading comprehension skills and vocabulary through the use of a structured cloze format, a process that allows children to choose words to fill in blanks of a paragraph. This cloze format focuses on meaning completion, vocabulary in context, or syntax development. These aid a teacher in assessing a student's ability to work with semantic and syntactic clues, which in turn can help a teacher to place a student in the appropriate reading level.

A paragraph is given to the child with blanks inserted in the middle of sentences, where words should be. The child is given a list of five words from which to choose, and must pick the best one. This format gives children choices and allows them to make decisions for themselves. Children may choose clues that have pertinent information about the correct word. This will help a child pick the correct answer, develop a vocabulary, and show that some words have the same meaning. For example, the correct word in a sentence might be "cut;" a clue word could be "slice." After two wrong responses, the correct answer is given, along with explanatory information about what the child did wrong. Next, positive reinforcement is given to the child, upon a chosen correct answer. Lastly, a child will receive a summary of their performance.

Bailey's Book House
Edmark
P.O. Box 97021
Redmond, Washington 98073

Bailey's Book House is a CD-ROM computer program that is designed to help children ages 2-6 learn and enjoy reading. The interactive program offers different areas or "rooms" in which children can learn various aspects of the written language. There is a "letter machine" where children can both see and hear a letter articulated. It is followed by an interactive demonstration by an object beginning with that particular letter. There is a "read a rhyme" room where the children can work on phrases that include rhyming words and their different meanings despite the fact that they sound similar. Another room allows them to work on the meanings of the different prepositions. The children are asked to direct a trick dog in different directions in relation to his dog house. When they click on the correct word, the dog goes where he was directed and repeats again for the child where he is in relation to the house. The last room in Bailey's Book House is a "make a story room." In this room children are again given prompts which they fill in to create a story of their very own. As they continue writing the story, the finished prompts along with their pictures are collected. When the children are finished their story, they can choose to have Bailey read it back to them, or they can print out the story and share it with the class.

This product is appropriate for an educationally handicapped child because it breaks down the task of reading into smaller, more manageable parts. This program would be especially effective if the child was having problems with basic reading skills. If the child is having trouble reading because he/she cannot tell "b" and "d" apart, that is where you need to begin teaching the child. The program is also interactive which would continually redirect the child's attention to the monitor.

It is virtually impossible to be unsuccessful at writing a story in Bailey's Book House! After children have successfully created stories of their own with Bailey's help, they can move on to attempting a story by themselves.

Author's Birthday
Living Books
Broderbund Software for Education
500 Redwood Blvd.
Novato, California 94948

The Living Books series on CD-ROM which includes Author's Birthday was created to help young children learn and enjoy reading. Author's Birthday can be read in either English or Spanish, which would be extremely beneficial for an English as a second language child. The pages of the book offer an interactive introduction to reading. Upon beginning the book, the child is first read the page by a narrator that clearly articulates all of the words. As the narrator reads the words, they light up so that the child can follow along. After the page has been read, the child can "play" inside the page by simply clicking on various pictures. From inside the page the children can choose to have the page reread to them or they can simply click on the words to have them repeated. When beginning the program you can choose to work through the whole book or you can go directly to a specific page to work.

Since educationally handicapped children are such a diverse group of students, different aspects of this program fit the varying needs of students. If a child is having problems reading they are most likely also having problems in other language areas. Many of the benefits this program offers to reading, also benefits other language problems that may co-exist.

This program can also be used to help those children who are having problems in a specific area of reading. The program allows you to cue the book to a particular page and then work within that page. If after task analysis the teacher finds the child is having problems with verbs, the teacher can cue the book to a page that deals with verbs. Children can fill out a work sheet using the verbs they find within the story.

The program is good at articulating and presenting material to the user. The words are clearly pronounced for the child who is having problems reading because of language problems. The flow of reading the English language is also modeled for the children. If a child has hearing or learning problems that contribute to the reading problem, the book gives them a chance to first listen for meaning and then listen again for comprehension.

Listening Corner
Houghton-Mifflin Company
1 Beacon Street
Boston, Massachusettes 02108

Listening Corner is an audiocassette program using adults and children's voices with a variety of "skill" songs, to reinforce and enrich vocabulary and reading skills. It comes with worksheets focusing on vocabulary, phonics, and comprehension.

It is good for students who are slow readers who can now take their time reading, because they can stop the tape whenever they wish. The program includes "skills" concepts in reading, and it is designed to be used with the Houghton-Mifflin reading books.

It is appropriate with oral learners and slow readers or those just learning to read, because they can proceed at their own pace, without being rushed by the progress of other students. It also comes with vocabulary and reading skills activities.

Reading Skill Builder
Reader's Digest Services
Pleasantville, New York 10570

The main features of this program include a twenty-four volume series of stories which help the student to build on their reading skills as well as their language skills. These books reinforce twenty-two major reading skills and vocabulary skills. Each story ends with questions which help with the skill of reading comprehension. There is also a teachers guide provided so that either the students or the teacher can correct the answers following the activity.

These books focus mainly on comprehension and vocabulary and emphasize skills of listening and observation and encourage evaluation and interpretation.

This product can be considered appropriate for the educationally handicapped because it provides interesting stories that get the attention of the reader and keep it. These books allow for group work as well as for individual work. They also allow the teacher to see where the student is having difficulties and where the student needs some individual work. There are key words provided at the beginning of each of the stories which help with vocabulary and the questions at the end help with comprehension.

Phonics Review
School Zone
P.O. Box 777
Grand Haven, MI 49417

This product contains fifty-five cards which contain one or more pictures and a word representing a phonetic sound. The other side of the card has a list of additional words including the same sound.

The main features of this product are worksheets containing basic phonetic sounds including short and long vowel sounds, letter combinations, silent letters, contractions, compound words, plural endings, suffixes, and prefixes. It also includes an answer key in the back of the book.

These cards help the student to learn phonetic sounds which a student must master in order to learn how to read. The cards represent a large number of phonetic sounds and allow the students to have fun while teaming. The flip side of the card allows the student to relate what he has teamed to other commonly used words. This allows the student to reinforce what he has teamed from the first side of the card. The strengths of this product are that it includes many of the different skills in order to learn how to read. This allows the student to practice the skills that they have learned and the answer key in the back allows them to check their own work.

One reason this product is appropriate for the educationally handicapped children is because teachers can make the pace much slower and continue to review until the student has mastered the sound.

LANGUAGE ARTS RESOURCES

Kids Works Deluxe
Davidson & Associates, Inc.
P.O. Box 2961
Torrance, California 90509

Kids Works Deluxe is a multimedia program that combines a word processor and paint program to create a great adventure while learning. This is an appropriate and popular "first" word processor. It is an ideal way to build reading, writing, and creativity skills. This program assists children in creating stories, letters, journals, and more. It paints so children can create animated illustrations and talks so children can hear their stories read back to them. There are also many great tools such as animated stamps and interesting sound effects. Therefore, children have endless opportunities to express themselves through words, pictures, and sounds.

This program makes building writing skills fun. It is an interactive program, allows children to become involved in learning, and encourages children to develop creativity skills along with building writing skills. Another feature of this program is that it allows children to work at their own pace. For children with reading difficulties, you can insert pictures to replace words. This program reads the story back to you, which would also be beneficial to an educationally handicapped child.

Kid Works Deluxe would be likely to keep a child's attention because it actively involves them in learning. It uses task analysis and breaks the writing process down into its component parts. It takes you step by step through the writing process. In this program it is possible to replace words with pictures. This may be very beneficial to the educationally handicapped child who has problems reading. Also, after writing a story, a child can have it read back to them. This can be useful in helping children check their work.

Write: Outloud
Don Johnston, Inc.
P.O. Box 639
Wauconda, Illinois 60083

The Write: Outloud program is designed to allow students with any type of disability in language to hear their work as it is being typed. The user can listen to each letter, word, sentence, or paragraph as it is being typed, depending on the student's needs. The spell check is programmed to read the misspelled word in the sentence, isolate the word, and then spell it correctly; moreover, it offers a list of alternatively spelled words and can read and spell the list as well. The program provides an on-screen auditory toolbar to allow the student to both hear and see what needs to be done when help is needed. Another feature is that the software's spoken voice can be changed to suit the specific needs or preferences of the child. The program is capable of importing written documents from other word processor programs and placing them into the format of Write: Outloud.

This program is appropriate for educationally handicapped students because all of these features help the child to better understand language by both simultaneously hearing and seeing the process of writing occur. Likewise, the child is able to become more independent because he will require increasingly less help with his work, and he is likely to gain a sense of accomplishment when the work is finished.

Co:Writer
Don Johnston, Inc.
P.O. Box 639
Wauconda, Illinois 60083

Co:Writer is a useful tool in facilitating writing in students. The program predicts words for the writer based on what has already been written. It enables this to happen by thinking ahead and considering subject-verb agreements, grammar rules, user preferences and word relationships. There are three different levels of "dictionary sizes" for the student to determine at what efficiency and skill level the program can be used. It can also learn new words if desired. In addition, this program provides auditory feedback for those children with any types of language or hearing impairments. The only weakness with this program is that it could possibly become a crutch to students who use it often because they may rely too heavily on it to spell difficult words for them.

This program is appropriate for educationally handicapped children because it makes it easier for students to complete their thoughts when writing and promotes self-confidence because of speedier success. It is especially good for students with learning disabilities because they oftentimes have trouble turning their thoughts into written word. It also takes into consideration the hearing impaired by allowing for the option of auditory feedback. However, Co: Writer should be carefully prescribed by parents and teachers because the students could easily fall into using it as a crutch for spelling problems or word arrangement.

Syntaxercises
Communication Builders
3830 E. Bellevue
P.O. Box 42050
Tucson, Arizona 85733

Syntaxercises are language games for syntax practice. It includes game boards and components for two to four individuals to play five language games. Each is designed to elicit correct syntax production of a specific structure through participation in game format. The five games are: Pronoun Playground, Verb Voyage, Adjective Antics, Adverb Derby, and Question Mansion.

Syntaxercises prepares children to gain a better understanding of sequencing and combination of words for creating sentences. This game is excellent for those who need extra practice in picking out the correct parts of the sentence and word order. Each sentence structure is a different game. This allows for the student to concentrate on one area of difficulty at a time. Having five different games enables the child to experience a new dimension of the words and sentences without getting bored. The child can then reach an instructional level that he has not fully comprehended. These activities emphasize the importance of using language in social interactions. The players experience sharing information, initiating conversations, and maintaining the topic of conversation. Syntaxercises can be used as a learning center or as a free-time reinforcement activity.

Kid Pix
Broderbund Software
P.O. Box 6125
Novato, California 94948-6125

The various capabilities of Kid Pix allow the teacher to use it to replace flash cards and board games. It is a program which starts with the most basic concepts in reading and language development such as sound/letter correspondence and eventually culminates with the students creating stories with pictures. Kid Pix attacks the specifics, such as simple sentences and certain sounds and concepts which a teacher might be trying to help the student learn. It results in the student creating a story which he/she can save and keep in his/her assessment portfolio to show the progress made over time. This program may be reinforcing because it combines audio with video in helping the student to understand certain concepts. It helps the students focus their attention more because they are using a computer interactively and not just listening to a teacher. Assuming that the child is capable of using a computer, this program is appropriate because it encourages students to try by asking the most simple tasks and building up to more difficult tasks. It will almost definitely have one area in which the student can excel, and this will reinforce the child and give him/her the courage to tackle a more difficult area. Kid Pix is very motivational because it incorporates words, pictures, and sound, and children can also apply themselves to take their projects further by using this program.

Appendix B

MATHEMATICS RESOURCES FOR
EDUCATIONALLY HANDICAPPED STUDENTS

MATHEMATICS RESOURCES

Number-Rama
Incentive Publications, Inc.
Nashville, Tennessee

Number-Rama is a bulletin board that teaches numerals and number concepts. The numbers are enlarged and jumbled using a variety of colors and patterns.

This activity is appropriate for educationally handicapped children because even from the start the many different colors, patterns and sizes used on the board should attract the students' attention. Another reason is that it is a large visual, or example of spatial intelligence, that will help the students understand the concept. The way that this bulletin board may used in a lesson is to center oral recognition activities around the board. The teacher may instruct the class to point to all of the threes, or see how many sixes they can find. Another way to use the board is to point to the number and have the students tell you the names of the numbers, or have the class name each numeral.

Big: Calc
Don Johnston, Inc.
P.O. Box 639
Wauconda, Illinois 60083

Big: Calc is a software program that has many key features and educational benefits. The program is especially created for students with special needs. There are different calculator layouts which include a business calc, giant calc, keyboard, number line, phone pad, and a pyramid. Math equations can be arranged vertically or horizontally. Speech options are included, which allows the students to hear the numbers, functions or the entire equation as they type them in. The voice on the speech options, color, background, font, and font size can be changed to accommodate student preferences. A touchscreen can be attached and used with this program which can help children with motor problems.

Big: Calc would be well-used with an educationally handicapped student, especially students with auditory and motor disabilities. This program would be especially helpful with students in a first-grade class. They can be learning basic equations such as $1 + 1 = 2$, and the student can hear the numbers and symbols as they type them on the computer. Because the equation will also be read back to them at the end of the equation, the students can recognize the numbers along with their sounds. Students who have a disability with motor skills can use a touchscreen on the computer to do the same things as the rest of the students. This program allows the students to become familiar with computers and also have individual attention from the computer.

Counting on Frank
Gareth Stevens Publishing
1555 North River Center Drive
Milwaukee, Wisconsin 53212

Counting on Frank is a book that involves math and is a short story of the wild imagination of a boy and his dog, Frank. The boy figures out many problems by using facts and figures. This book is superb for introducing math concepts. It allows the students to use their imagination and learn at the same time. There are many realistic examples that the students can easily identify and understand. For example, the boy figured out that it would take 24 Franks to fill up his bedroom. At the end of the book, there are several activities which the students can attempt to complete on their own. The answers are also listed in back of the book. The questions make the student think and use different types of math (addition, subtraction, etc.). This book makes math fun.

Counting on Frank would be excellent for educationally handicapped students, and it will maintain the students attention because it is a very entertaining book. The students will likely enjoy math more because they can relate it to things in their life and things at home. The book allows the students to use their imagination and also expand their thinking skills. It exposes students to the metric system, as well as measurement, counting, addition, subtraction, multiplication, and word problems.

Manipulative Starter Kit
Cuisenaire Company of America, Inc.
10 Bank Street
PO Box 5026
White Plains, New York 10602-5026

The Manipulative Starter Kit includes a resource book, color cubes, two-color counters, fraction circles, cuisenaire rods, overhead pattern blocks, dice, mirrors, overhead base of ten blocks, tangram, and a geoboard. The kit is designed to introduce new math concepts to a wide range of grades, (kindergarten to eighth-grade) and it allows students to have hands-on experience with the concepts. The manipulatives in the kit allow the teacher to teach the lesson as the students are able to experiment freely and figure out the problems by themselves. The kit can be used for problem solving, fraction, probability, geometry, measurement, games, and patterns.

Ten-Tens Counting Frame
Milton Bradley, Company
Springfield, Massachusetts

The purpose of this product is to assist in the understanding of counting and understanding number relationships. The main feature of this product is a frame with ten rods running horizontally across the frame. Each rod contains ten colored beads.

This product has many strengths including the fact that it serves as a physical manipulative. The students are able to see the relationships numbers have, as well as be able to understand simple addition and subtraction. In addition, Ten-Tens Couting Frame is durable, easy to use, and can enhance a variety of math lessons. It can be used to aid in teaching simple addition, simple subtraction, place values, and simple multiplication. This product is not something that can be used only during certain lessons; rather, it can be applied to many.

Grocery Cart
Creative Teaching Associates
P.O. Box 7766
Fresno, California 93747

The main purpose of the game Grocery Cart is to teach and reinforce the skills of counting money. The game focuses on the everyday activity of grocery shopping, and introduces the skill of counting money. The children are familiar with this activity, therefore when counting and exchanging money becomes the focus of the lesson, the children will feel comfortable in the situation in which it is introduced.

The main features of this product are the Grocery Cart game board, coupons, play dollars and coins, sale circulars, and nine copies of different shopping lists. Using these tools, students will simulate a grocery shopping experience and be responsible for budgeting the money the have been given to spend.

This game has many strengths, and the fact that it is presented as a game will increase the attentiveness of the students. The students are given a certain amount of play dollars in a variety of denominations. This physical manipulative, the play money, allows the children to handle what they are learning about, rather than looking at pictures of money in a text book, as well as see what they are computing. Another strength of this game is that it requires the students to compare prices in different sales circulars to see where they would save the most money.

Cuisenaire Rods
Cuisenaire Company of America Inc.
12 Church Street
New Rochelle, New York 10805

Cuisenaire rods are manipulatives which can be used to teach mathematics to students at any grade level, even in secondary education. Cuisenaire rods are three-dimensional rectangular objects of different lengths. Each rod is color-coded according to length. All of the rods are referred to by the first letter of the color, except the blue, black, and brown rods, which are denoted according to the last letter. Cuisenaire rods are not simply blocks; rather, because they have the same properties as numbers, are symbols for numbers.

Cuisenaire rods help students to understand the relationship among numbers through the aid of manipulatives. Even though Cuisenaire rods appear to be for elementary mathematics, they are also useful in secondary mathematics. Not only are they used for addition and subtraction, but they can also serve as an introduction to symbolic thinking, which is used in the specific areas of algebra and geometry.

Cuisenaire rods are appropriate for all educationally handicapped children. Educationally handicapped students do not use abstractions well, and Cuisenaire rods provide concrete examples to help develop these concepts.

Coordinated Cross-Number Puzzles
McCormick-Mathers Publishing Company, Inc.
Cincinnati, Ohio 45202

The Coordinated Cross-Number Puzzles are like regular crossword puzzles. However, instead of words as answers to clues, this program requires answers to math problems. Each workbook contains a series of puzzles which corresponds to most math textbooks. The workbooks can be selected according to the level of math of each individual.

Many students are interested in puzzles, and therefore, these worksheets have the natural ability to motivate students to do math. Secondly, because this type of math worksheet differs from traditional math drills, the puzzles provide which may lead to interest and stimulation. Also, because the answers intersect one another, the answers are self-checking. The students will most likely know if they did the problems correctly. Another advantage of using this workbook is that each puzzle corresponds to the content in most basic math textbooks.

INDEX

CHARLES C THOMAS • PUBLISHER, LTD.

- Malouff, John & Nicola Schutte—**GAMES TO ENHANCE SOCIAL AND EMOTIONAL SKILLS: Sixty-Six Games that Teach Children, Adolescents, and Adults Skills Crucial to Success in Life**. '98, 130 pp. (8 1/2 x 11), 3 il., spiral (paper).

- Hollis, James N.—**CONDUCTING INDIVIDUALIZED EDUCATION PROGRAM MEETINGS THAT WITHSTAND DUE PROCESS: The Informal Evidentiary Proceeding**. '98, 174 pp. (7 x 10).

- Walsh, William M. & G. Robert Williams—**SCHOOLS AND FAMILY THERAPY: Using Systems Theory and Family Therapy in the Resolution of School Problems**. '97, 236 pp. (7 x 10), 2 il., 5 tables, $47.95, cloth, $34.95, paper.

- Fryburg, Estelle L.—**READING AND LEARNING DISABILITY: A Neuropsychological Approach to Evaluation and Instruction**. '97, 398 pp. (7 x 10), 13 il., 9 tables, $79.95, cloth, $64.95, paper.

- Bush, Janet—**THE HANDBOOK OF SCHOOL ART THERAPY: Introducing Art Therapy Into a School System**. '97, 206 pp. (7 x 10), 26 il., $48.95, cloth, $35.95, paper.

- Shade, Barbara J.—**CULTURE, STYLE AND THE EDUCATIVE PROCESS: Making Schools Work for Racially Diverse Students. (2nd Ed.)** '97, 264 pp. (7 x 10), 4 il., 1 table, $57.95, cloth, $42.95, paper.

- Harlan, Joan C.—**BEHAVIOR MANAGEMENT STRATEGIES FOR TEACHERS: Achieving Instructional Effectiveness, Student Success, and Student Motivation—Every Teacher and Any Student Can**. '96, 292 pp. (7 x 10), $55.95, cloth, $39.95, paper.

- English, Fenwick W. & Robert L. Larson—**CURRICULUM MANAGEMENT FOR EDUCATIONAL AND SOCIAL SERVICE ORGANIZATIONS. (2nd Ed.)** '96, 286 pp. (7 x 10), 8 il., 6 tables, $59.95, cloth, $41.95, paper.

- Phillips, Norma Kolko & S. Lala Ashenberg Straussner—**CHILDREN IN THE URBAN ENVIRONMENT: Linking Social Policy and Clinical Practice**. '96, 258 pp. (7 x 10), 2 il., 1 table, $60.95, cloth, $46.95, paper.

- Grossman, Herbert—**EDUCATING HISPANIC STUDENTS: Implications for Instruction, Classroom Management, Counseling and Assessment. (2nd Ed.)** '95, 290 pp. (7 x 10), 17 tables, $60.95, cloth, $40.95, paper.

- Rich, John Martin & Joseph L. DeVitis—**THEORIES OF MORAL DEVELOPMENT. (2nd Ed.)** '94, 164 pp. (7 x 10), $36.95, cloth, $24.95, paper.

- Bushman, John H. & Kay Parks Bushman—**TEACHING ENGLISH CREATIVELY. (2nd Ed.)** '94, 254 pp. (7 x 10), 48 il., $50.95.

- Holley, Shelby—**A PRACTICAL PARENT'S HANDBOOK ON TEACHING CHILDREN WITH LEARNING DISABILITIES**. '94, 308 pp., 13 il., 1 table, $65.95, cloth, $41.95, paper.

- Grossman, Herbert—**ENDING DISCRIMINATION IN SPECIAL EDUCATION**. '98, 100 pp. (7 x 10), paper, $18.95.

- Hunt, Gilbert H., Dennis Wiseman & Sandra Bowden—**THE MIDDLE LEVEL TEACHERS' HANDBOOK: Becoming A Reflective Practitioner**. '98, 248 pp. (7 x 10), 39 il., 11 tables.

- Burns, Edward—**TEST ACCOMMODATIONS FOR STUDENTS WITH DISABILITIES**. '98, 272 pp. (7 x 10), 47 tables.

- Reglin, Gary—**MENTORING STUDENTS AT RISK: An Underutilized Alternative Education Strategy for K-12 Teachers**. '98, 110 pp. (7 x 10), 2 il., 1 table, $17.95, paper.

- Fairchild, Thomas N.—**CRISIS INTERVENTION STRATEGIES FOR SCHOOL-BASED HELPERS. (2nd Ed.)** '97, 496 pp. (7 x 10), 8 il., 12 tables, $109.95, cloth, $92.95, paper.

- Westmeyer, Paul—**AN ANALYTICAL HISTORY OF AMERICAN HIGHER EDUCATION. (2nd Ed.)** '97, 196 pp. (7 x 10), 1 il., $52.95, cloth $39.95 paper.

- Williamson, Deborah, Kevin I. Minor, & James W. Fox—**LAW-RELATED EDUCATION AND JUVENILE JUSTICE: Promoting Citizenship Among Juvenile Offenders**. '97, 284 pp. (7 x 10), 2 il., 6 tables, $59.95, cloth, $44.95, paper.

- Hargis, Charles H.—**TEACHING LOW ACHIEVING AND DISADVANTAGED STUDENTS. (2nd Ed.)** '97, 202 pp. (7 x 10), $36.95, paper.

- Kelly, Noeline Thompson & Brian John Kelly—**PHYSICAL EDUCATION FOR PRE-SCHOOL AND PRIMARY GRADES. (2nd. Ed.)** '97, 256 pp. (7 x 10) 124 il., $39.95, spiral (paper).

- Verduin, John R., Jr.—**HELPING STUDENTS DEVELOP INVESTIGATIVE, PROBLEM SOLVING, AND THINKING SKILLS IN A COOPERATIVE SETTING: A Handbook for Teachers, Administrators, and Curriculum Workers**. '96, 114 pp. (7 x 10), $31.95, cloth, $20.95, paper.

- Adams, Dennis & Mary Hamm—**COOPERATIVE LEARNING: Critical Thinking and Collaboration Across the Curriculum. (2nd Ed.)** '96, 294 pp. (7 x 10), 27 il., 1 table, $50.95, cloth, $34.95, paper.

- Hargis, Charles H.—**CURRICULUM BASED ASSESSMENT: A Primer. (2nd Ed.)** '95, 190 pp. (7 x 10), $33.95, paper

- Humphrey, James H.—**PHYSICAL EDUCATION FOR THE ELEMENTARY SCHOOL**. '94, 292 pp. (7 x 10), 8 il., $49.95, cloth, $35.95, paper.

- Burnsed, C. Vernon — **THE CLASSROOM TEACHER'S GUIDE TO MUSIC EDUCATION**. '93, 174 pp. (8 1/2 x 11), 131 il., $33.95, spiral (paper).

- Fuchs, Lucy—**HUMANITIES IN THE ELEMENTARY SCHOOL: A Handbook for Teachers**. '93, 140 pp. (7 x 10), $35.95, cloth, $24.95, paper.

Write, call 1-800-258-8980 or 1-217-789-8980 or FAX (217)789-9130 • www.ccthomas.com • books@ccthomas.com
Books sent on approval • $5.50 - Shipping / $6.50 - Canada • Prices subject to change without notice

2600 South First Street • Springfield • Illinois • 62704